DiddleDots

Tips to Ease
the Craziness
of Parenting

Susie Garlick

To Mike, Ryan, Macy & Kenzie...

Thank you for the simple gift of you.

Contents

• • •

A Note from Me

• • •

From the moment I started my DiddleDots website in 2009, I was always second-guessing myself. I will never forget the moment I sent my first DiddleDot into the cyber world. I stared at my computer and thought, "Oh no! What did I just do?" I was plagued by the question, "Who do you think you are to give parenting advice to others? You are raising three young children yourself." It was a question that always seemed to shut me down. How could I give parenting advice when I was dealing with parenting issues in my own life?

The DiddleDots website received wonderful feedback, but with the feedback came the pressure. People began sending emails that said, "Will you come to my house and raise my kids?" or "You have your life so together, how do you do it?" I felt as if I was painting a picture of myself that was far from who I was. My life was not "so" together. It was challenging enough raising my own kids, let alone someone else's. I was a mom trying my hardest, but making mistakes along the way. I stopped the website and DiddleDots found its way to a shelf where it began collecting dust.

As time passed, I found myself wanting to write a *DiddleDots* book. So back and forth I would go between working on this book and worrying about the pressure. One day a simple thought went through my mind, "Get over yourself. This book can help others." In that moment everything opened up.

I was the perfect one to share DiddleDots because I was in the middle of the craziness just like everyone else. My journey had brought me to this point for a specific reason. Everything I had gone through and experienced brought me the insight, the intuition and the inner drive to put these ideas into words. Does this make me a perfect parent? No. It makes me a parent desperate to find the right tools to solve whatever problems come my way. In doing so I not only help myself, but hopefully others as well.

This book is a collection of ideas I have learned and lived. They may or may not work for everyone, but they have worked for me. If I walk away from this experience knowing that I have helped in a small way, a big way or anyway at all, then I am glad that *DiddleDots* made its way off the shelf, out of the dust and into your lives.

Introduction

● ● ●

We all know what it takes to run a successful company or be a strong employee: hard work, organization and delegation. This should be the same in your home. You are the teacher of your classroom, the CEO of your family, the secretary of your office. You are in charge and if you fall apart, everything falls apart. Can you imagine if you walked into a meeting as the CEO of a company with nothing prepared? What about starting your day as a teacher with no lesson plans? How about botching up all the messages that clients left for your boss? How long do you think you would last in your position? Not very long!

Day after day, moms around the country start off with a tap, tap, tap from their children saying, "Wake up, I am hungry!" The day has started and nothing is prepared. Moms need to make sure everyone is dressed (including themselves), feed hungry bodies (including the dog), pack a different lunch for each child (as well as a snack and water bottle), make sure hair and teeth are brushed, see if backpacks are filled with homework from the night before, check if signatures are where they need to be and hope shoes are on the right feet and tied. The children are fighting, clothes are missing and milk is spilling all over the place. Moms run out the door with a sink full of dirty dishes (if they even make it that far), race to school and drop off the kids with a "Hurry, you are going to be late!" The kids are a wreck, the mom is stressed and it is only 8:00am.

There was a time in my life where this scenario was not that far-fetched. In what seems like the blink of an eye I had three children under the age of six and everything was spiraling out of control. Laundry was piled up all over the house, I could never find what I was looking for and showers were a rarity—I just wasn't happy.

Seven years earlier I had been a successful teacher running an organized, happy classroom of twenty-something first graders and now my small classroom of three seemed to be crumbling before my eyes. Where had I lost control and could I get any of my sanity back?

When I was working on my teaching degree, one of my professors told me the more classroom management I had the less behavioral problems I would deal with. If this worked in my classroom, why could it not work in my home? Things began to change. Along with help from family, friends and counselors I slowly began picking up the pieces of my life. I started bringing the techniques I had used as a teacher into my home and before I knew it the laundry was getting done, things were no longer lost, showers became a priority and I was happier. I had become a teacher again and although life was still crazy, it was not out of control.

We are parenting during a time like no other in history. Often, it feels as if someone hit the fast forward button and it stuck. We have become a nation obsessed with technology, fast food and quick fixes. We are over-scheduled, under-valued and exhausted. At the end of the day it is easier to watch reality television, read about others on Facebook or catch up on the latest Hollywood gossip than deal with our own lives. Like it our not, it is affecting our children.

Parents are doing their best to raise happy, healthy and respectful children, but society is making that very challenging. While it would be unfair to make a blanket statement, I do think it is fair to say that more and more children are throwing temper tantrums at older ages, dealing with depression and self-esteem issues and just looking unhappier than in generations past.

We as a society of parents need to fix the fast forward button and slow down. *DiddleDots* is a steppingstone in that direction. Back in 2009, I began DiddleDots as a website. I sent out one parenting tip a day and called these tips Dots. These Dots were not earth shattering but simple ideas to get parents thinking about how they were running their homes as well as their lives. The website was initially short lived, but I knew I would eventually publish a *DiddleDots* book. The question became, how could I organize the Dots to make them most helpful to parents?

I knew organization would be the first chapter. It is difficult to run any institution if it is disorganized and your home is no exception. I saw it first hand in my classroom and I now see it within my own home. Without an organized home it is difficult to teach expectations, deal with children's feelings or instill values. Once you are organized you have completed the first step toward a calmer, happier home.

The next step is teaching expectations. By teaching expectations, chapter two, you are not only making your life easier but you are helping your children learn the tools they need to survive in the real world. In the craziness of a day it is easy to forget that our job as parents is to teach our children how to be citizens of the world. Teaching expectations at an early age will do this.

The third chapter is on feelings. So much of parenting today concentrates on our children's feelings and self-esteem. Many parents believe that talking everything out and telling our children how wonderful they are will raise confident and caring children. This is simply not the case. While tapping into feelings is important and self-esteem is a goal for our children, we just might be doing it the wrong way. This chapter will give you ideas and insight into what works and what doesn't work when it comes to feelings.

The last chapter is on values. This chapter is not a way for me to instill my values on you. It is a way for you to look at what is valuable in your own life. So often we fly through life too busy to notice the passing day. Taking time to reevaluate your values is a wonderful way to slow down and appreciate the small things in life—your children.

As you begin reading *DiddleDots*, remember that this is not a book with in-depth answers. These are Dots to get you thinking. Between my Bachelor of Arts in Elementary Education, my work toward a Master of Arts in Professional Counseling and being a parent, I have bookshelves filled with advice from professionals across the board. I have incorporated some of these resources within the book and listed them under References & Recommendations at the back of the book. Use them if you would like to learn more.

If you are feeling helpless or out of control, you will need more than this book has to offer. When I was down and out I sought the help I needed and I am a better mom, wife and person because of it. Please remember that seeking help is not a sign of weakness. It is the complete opposite. Getting the help you need is a sign of strength. There are times in life that we can't solve our own problems and that is when we turn to people who have the background and knowledge that we don't. If not for yourself, do it for your children.

In the blink of an eye our children grow up. It is my hope that in that blink we will have raised humans who are contributing to this world in a positive way. What a wonderful world it would be.

DiddleDots

Tips to Ease
the Craziness
of Parenting

Organization

• • •

1

What Happened to My Home?

• • •

Not too long ago, I looked around my home and was sure that a giant had picked it up, shook it and walked away leaving everything misplaced and disheveled. I am not prone to anxiety attacks, but this almost put me over the edge. I took a deep breath and tried to regain my composure.

When I began breathing normally, I made a list of every space in my house: the master bedroom, the master bathroom, the master closet, the kitchen, the office, the hall closet, the playroom, etc. You get the idea. I took out my planner and scheduled time to organize each space in my home. It was then time to begin.

I started in my master closet. I took everything off the shelves and out of the drawers—my closet was completely empty and my floor was completely covered with a sea of clothes, shoes and accessories. I then placed everything into three different piles: donate, sell and things to throw away. Everything that was left I reorganized and placed back onto the shelves and into the drawers.

When you begin this process you must follow one rule: Do not buy anything you want, only buy the things you need. There is nothing worse than going through this process only to find that the spaces you already cleaned are disorganized again.

The things we surround ourselves with should make us happy whereas too much stuff can overwhelm us. The more simple and organized our lives, the better we will be as parents. I know it seems like a strange correlation, but it is true. You will quickly see that organization will bring you one step closer to calm.

2

Things to Save

● ● ●

What to save? This is a question that overwhelms parents and we find ourselves asking, "Should I save this or toss it and if I toss it will my child be devastated for the rest of his life?" The answer to my sarcastic questions is no! Let me remind you that too much "stuff" can weigh you down, so why weigh your children down with things they will need to deal with someday?

When it comes to paperwork, I have a drawer that simply says, "Things to Save." It seems like I open it every day and stick something into the glorious pile of papers. When the drawer fills up, it is my cue that it is time to deal with the monster. I make three piles, one for each of my children. I then take one pile at a time and separate it into little groups: artwork, schoolwork, achievements (certificates, awards, ribbons), letters, school pictures, invitations, report cards, etc.

From this pile I make sure to save the things that are unique and tell a story about my child. I then recycle the rest. Buy a notebook, a set of dividers and page protectors and number the dividers by years.

Take your small pile, put them into pocket protectors and place them under the corresponding year. For example, under my son's 6th year I have his birthday invitation, two pictures from his party, his kindergarten report card, his school picture, his team soccer picture, three pieces of artwork, a certificate he earned in school, some of his first writing assignments and a letter from me. The process begins again when I place something new into the "Things to Save" drawer.

When your children are grown, they will be thrilled when you hand them a well organized notebook representing their life instead of handing them boxes full of crunched up papers that you never took the time to go through.

3

Clothes for Quilts

• • •

How many of you have a box of your children's clothes from their first years of life? How many of you can't bring yourself to get rid of them—any of them? If you are like me you might find yourself saying, "Look at this one. This is the shirt he wore when he said his first word. I must save this." Or, "This is the dress she was wearing when she went on her first airplane ride. I could never get rid of this!" If I could steal some texting talk—OMG! Although I had great intentions, I could have clothed an entire country of toddlers if it wasn't for my emotional attachments. While saving certain pieces is important, saving them all is insanity!

Take a deep breath—it's time to make three piles: donate, save and "grubbies." The first two are self-explanatory. Decide what you want to save and decide what you want to donate. The third pile is for "grubbies." These are the onsies, tee-shirts, leggings and jammies that you adore, but they are too grubby to donate or save. Bag them up and take them to a seamstress. Ask her to cut the clothes into little squares and sew them into a quilt.

You now have a darling keepsake with the memories of those precious, first years. Any time you can recycle your memories to use in your life, you have saved yourself another dusty box in the attic and you have filled your home with memories that will last a lifetime.

4

Masterpieces

● ● ●

When you walk into any elementary school classroom the students' work covers the walls. If I were to cover the walls of our home with our children's artwork, we would have enough to start a wallpapering business. For this reason I have designated spots for the kids' artwork.

We have a humongous bulletin board covered with our children's "Masterpieces." When artwork comes home, I take an old piece off the board and tack the new one on the board. After a couple weeks in the spotlight it is much easier to decide if it is a keeper or heading for the trash. There is nothing worse than taking something out of your child's backpack and throwing it away, only to have your child in tears when it's found crumpled at the bottom of the garbage. By placing the artwork on the board it gets the attention it deserves for the moment and, usually, by the next day that piece is old news.

Your child's artwork is a wonderful way to decorate your house while at the same time, it gives children a sense that what they create is unique and appreciated.

If you just can't stomach throwing away your children's artwork, try taking a picture of each piece throughout the year, store them in a digital file and then make an online photo book to buy. There are many online photo companies making amazing, personalized photo books that you will cherish forever.

5

Our Second Home

• • •

I have always dreamed of a second home, but recently I realized I have one—it is my car. If I were to add up the amount of time I spend in my car, it would probably be more than the amount of time I spend in my home or with my husband.

Have you ever heard that you can tell a woman's personality by looking in her purse? I think the same is true about our cars. When my car is a mess, my life seems to follow the same pattern. If my car is clean, my life is much more organized. Therefore, it would make sense to organize your car.

Get yourself a car basket. This should fit either in your front seat or on the floor. Fill it with small necessities: Band-aids©, Kleenex©, wipies, antibacterial gel, spare change, etc. During the day, while driving around, fill the basket with paperwork, purchases and garbage. At the end of the day, instead of having a car filled with the day's activities, you have it contained in one place. Take the basket inside, empty it out and re-stock it for the next day.

We must not forget the other occupants of our second home—our children. Explain to your children how you expect them to treat the car. When they leave the car they must take their things with them or their things will be donated. If your children leave garbage in the car, call them back and have them go through it again.

When our home is disorganized and dirty, it brings us down. The same is true of our cars. Clean your car everyday and enjoy your drive a little bit more.

6

The Food Notebook

● ● ●

Grocery shopping, meal planning, cooking, snacks, nutrition—anything having to do with food is so challenging for me. I love eating healthy. I have dreams of my children eating healthy. But, somehow I make myself crazy in the process. Three children, two adults, food allergies and stubbornness make feeding a family of five downright exhausting.

Buy a notebook and a set of notebook dividers. Divide the notebook into six sections: Kid's Menus, Breakfast Recipes, Lunch Recipes, Dinner Recipes, Snacks and Weekly Planning.

Sit down with each of your children and have them make a list of the things they like for breakfast, lunch, dinner and snacks. Place this list behind the tab "Kid's Menus." Making these lists does two things: one, it gives you an idea of what to stock the pantry with and two, when your children are indecisive about what they want to fix for themselves they can look at their list.

Next, look through recipe books, Internet sites and family recipes. Make copies of different meals you like and put them behind the corresponding tab: Breakfast Recipes, Lunch Recipes, Dinner Recipes and Snacks. Instead of looking through recipe books for your favorite meals, you have them available all the time.

The last section is "Weekly Planning." Fill it with plain paper and write out your meal plan for each week. Go through your recipes, check your pantry and write down the foods you need to buy. You might forget something here and there, but planning ahead of time will generally save you from those last minute trips to the grocery store to buy that one missing ingredient. With one less thing to worry about in the day you save time as well as grief.

7

Leftovers on Wednesdays

• • •

I can't tell you how many times I have been sitting around with my kids and find myself thinking, "What should I prepare for dinner?" This would be alright if I was planning dinner for the next night, but this thought usually comes to me about thirty minutes before I am supposed to be nourishing five bodies.

It is time to schedule your meals. Sit down and decide what Monday through Sunday will look like at dinnertime. Here is what a week might look like: Monday: cook, Tuesday: cook, Wednesday: leftovers, Thursday: kids cook, Friday: order out, Saturday: date night and Sunday: barbecue. Grab your food notebook and fill in what you need to buy for the week.

By planning this ahead of time you know what to expect, your family knows what to expect and you can plan accordingly.

8

Do You Know Where Your Scissors Are?

• • •

Do you know where your scissors are? How about your pencils, pencil sharpener, tape, glue, stapler, markers, crayons, lined paper and plain white paper? When I was teaching every child knew where everything was. It made the day run smoothly.

In our home we spend hours at our kitchen island. This is where my children do their homework, their arts and crafts, their board games, their puzzles, their chatting and their snacking. In one of the kitchen drawers I keep the pencils, pencil sharpener, tape, glue and stapler. In the middle of the island I have a white wooden box that has a jar filled with crayons, another one for colored pencils and still another for markers. The lined and plain white paper is in a drawer off of the kitchen.

When my children walk in the door to do their homework they can find anything they need to complete their assignments. There is nothing more frustrating than hearing, "Mom, where is a pencil?" I don't know about you, but homework time is busy time. I am going through backpacks, emptying lunchboxes, fixing snacks all while maneuvering through homework questions—I don't want to search the house for a pencil.

Choose a place for all the homework necessities and keep them organized and stocked. It is amazing how looking for something as small as a pencil can seem like a huge problem when you are busy.

9

Lesson Plans

• • •

When school is out, together time begins. The last week of school I can hardly wait for no structure, no schedules and no early mornings. One week after summer vacation has started I wonder what I was thinking the week before. The reality is that we as moms still have the same workload, but we have extra bodies to deal with. So while no early mornings are wonderful, we still need some structure and routine.

One of the best pieces of advice I learned as a teacher was, "The more classroom management you have, the less behavior problems you will deal with." In other words, the more you are prepared and organized, the smoother your day will run. Every day that your child enters the classroom, his teacher has prepared lesson plans. During summer vacation you are your child's teacher, so it is time to prepare your lessons.

As a school teacher, my lesson plans included the daily curriculum, quiet reading time, recess, lunch, free time and extra classes like P.E., art or music. I had one class scheduled as my free period that I could use for more preparation or my own personal use. From the moment my students walked into the classroom the schedule was on the board. While school will always be more structured than summer vacation, it is still a good idea to have some sort of plan.

Schedule the day before your kids wake up, let them know the plan and begin the day. If they aren't going to camp, fill their day with reading, games, outside time, quiet time, free choice, arts and crafts, lunch, chores and time for yourself. Will the schedule go exactly according to plan? Probably not, but that is okay. As long as there is a plan, your day will run much more smoothly than if you were winging it.

10
The Husband Table

● ● ●

In honor of all the dads out there I thought it would be nice to give them a gift. It is the "Husband Table." When my husband comes home from work his pockets are filled with keys, change, business cards and receipts. Before I created the "Husband Table" his items were everywhere. Now, by the back door we have a small table. On it sits a basket and a mail carrier. At night he empties his pockets in the basket and in the morning he refills his pockets with what he needs for the day. In the mail carrier, I put any mail that needs to go with him to his office.

It is such a simple idea, yet one that both my husband and I love. I don't find his emptied pockets all over the house and he doesn't have a nagging wife.

11

Timer Time

• • •

There is no better purchase than a timer. Timers can be used to help you organize your home and, more importantly, teach your children responsibility. I am a huge fan of taking the blame off of moms and shifting the responsibility to the children. A timer is the perfect tool for this. Pick a task you expect your child to do, tell him the amount of time he has to complete the task and set the timer. Be very clear that when the timer goes off your child needs to have completed the task or he will have a consequence. By setting the timer you are no longer the bad guy, the timer is. You can use a timer for anything: television, taking turns, reading, quiet time, cleaning, etc. Set the timer and when it rings, time is up. It is a simple, clear and effective way to teach responsibility.

12

Cardio Cleanup

• • •

I could clean all day if I didn't stop myself. That is why "Cardio Cleanup" is such an important part of my day. It forces me to clean for a set amount of time and then, believe it or not, stop.

"Cardio Cleanup" begins when I set the timer. I head to the back of my house with a garbage bag and a laundry basket and I start. As fast as I can, I empty the garbage, make the beds, grab my laundry, open the curtains and shades, unload the dishwasher, reload it, wipe off the countertops, do a quick sweep and start the laundry. I do all of this in 25-30 minutes. When the timer goes off I am done and I force myself to stop. My surface cleaning is done and my day can begin.

I am convinced there is something psychological that happens to our brains when our home is picked up. Less home clutter somehow makes our brain less cluttered. The added bonus is the faster you move, the higher your heart rate and the more exercise you get. Who would have thought that picking up could second as exercise?

One of the best websites I have ever found for cleaning and organizing tips is www.flylady.net. It is filled with wonderful ideas to keep your house in tip-top shape.

13

Holiday Cards

● ● ●

Do you ever wonder what to do with all the holiday cards you receive during the month of December? If you are like me there is a humongous guilt that comes with throwing them away. In the past I would bag them up in hopes that "someday" I would put them into wonderful picture books to see each family as they had grown through the years.

A few years back I realized I had ten bags of holiday cards collecting dust and taking up space. I had not made any picture books; I had no time to make picture books; and I had not looked at any of the pictures since the day we received them in the mail. I have finally come to the realization that it would cost me all our children's college education money, months of work and way too much stress to put together picture books that I would not have time to look at anyway.

That was when I bought a beautiful, large tray that sits in the middle of our dining room table. It sits there 365 days a year and it is filled with the previous year's holiday cards. When we have guests over they look at them; when my kids are eating a snack at the table they look at them; and when I have a free minute I look at them. They get looked at more in a year than my bagged cards did in ten years! At the beginning of the holiday season, I throw out the cards from the previous year to make room for the new cards. As they say, out with the old and in with the new.

14

Lots-o'-Socks

• • •

I can't tell you the number of times I have found one sock here, there and everywhere. One day I looked down to see my daughter wearing two different socks. I asked if she was starting a trend and she replied, "No, I couldn't find a pair that went together."

Someday, we will come to find out that there really is a black hole sucking all of our socks into another world; but, until then, try to keep as many matching socks together as possible. Buy some sort of container and place it in your laundry room. Every time you do wash place the solo socks into it. When it fills up, pull them out, match the ones you can and get rid of the rest. I know it seems simple, but if they don't go somewhere, they will end up everywhere.

15

Out of Sight, Out of Mind

• • •

How many times have you come home from a birthday party, fast food restaurant or carnival to have a pile of little plastic toys that break after one use? To us these toys are a nuisance, but to the kids they are treasures, at least for a day.

After one day of playing with these toys it is time to put them in a special place. Get a basket and place it high in a closet. This is your "Out of Sight, Out of Mind" basket. After the kids go to sleep put the toys there. Usually, the kids will forget about their treasures and a week later you can dispose of them. If they want them the next day, give them back and then try again. This whole process does two things: it helps clear out your house and it saves you from dealing with a humongous meltdown when your child sees you throwing away his special treasure.

16

The Homework Box

• • •

When my two oldest kids were in early elementary school, they were very serious about doing their homework. After school they would sit down and begin right away. This was always when my youngest daughter decided it was time to talk as loud as she could and tell her brother and sister every detail from her day. While I thought her stories were darling, her older brother and sister did not.

This is when I decided to make a "Homework Box" just for her. It was a special box that only came out during homework time. In it I put different things that she liked: puzzles, coloring books and a white board with markers. I made sure to fill it with things that were age appropriate so I knew she would be capable of doing them without any help from me.

Once the big kids were done with their homework, I put her "Homework Box" away until the next day. This gave me more time to help my older children and gave my then three year old the feeling of being independent like her big brother and big sister.

17

Lost & Found

• • •

Our neighborhood is filled with children of all ages. Needless to say there are many times when kids come over and leave behind everything from shoes to sippy cups. There are also times my children come home from a neighbor's house wearing an entirely different outfit than they left our house wearing. We have enough stuff of our own, we do not need the neighborhood stuff as well.

That is why I have a "Lost & Found." Anything that is not ours goes into the box. It sits in a cabinet under the sink and when the box fills up it is time to empty it. I sort the items by families and then make deliveries. I can keep everything contained until it is time to make returns. Simple, easy and helpful.

18

The Donation Box

• • •

As I am sure you can tell at this point, I am a firm believer that less stuff equals less stress. This is why every home needs a "Donation Box." This should be big enough to fill with lots of items and be stored in the garage.

Once a week or once a month, walk through your house and find five items to donate. Place them in your donation box. Whenever your children grow out of their shoes, shorts or shirts, place them in your "Donation Box." When you buy a new item, donate an old item. Once the "Donation Box" is filled, take it to your local charity. You will keep your house cleaned out while helping others at the same time.

19

Grab and Go

● ● ●

Do your kids ever tell you they are starved right when you are walking out the door? In my house that seems to be an ongoing theme. This is when I created the "Grab and Go" basket.

Whether it is in your pantry, a cabinet or on the way out the door, designate a basket for snacks on the go. These should be somewhat healthy, pre-packaged snacks that your kids can grab on their way to school, when they need a quick bite after playing or to stick in their backpack for camp. If my kids are hungry and we are walking out the door, I tell them to grab a snack from the basket and they are good to go.

Having a "Grab and Go" basket allows our children to be in control of what they are eating, reinforces the importance of healthy snacks and is less stress for mom. When kids are running on low and need a little extra nutrition, a "Grab and Go" basket is a perfect solution to fill up their empty tanks.

20

Kids Say the Funniest Things

• • •

During the flu season, my then three year old announced that, "If you do not wear underwear, the flu germs will go up your tushy." Once I peeled myself off the floor from laughter, I immediately went to my "Favorite Quotes" book, wrote it down and dated it. Kids say the funniest things, but if you are anything like me you forget them as fast as they say them. I like to call it mommy amnesia. Buy yourself a journal, put it in an easily accessible place and enjoy the funny things your children say for the rest of your life.

21

The Magazine Mountain

• • •

A few years back, I found myself with a collection of magazines that was taking on a life of its own. The pile was ridiculous. I kept the magazines with the mentality that someday I would do the craft projects, cook all the recipes or use all the inspirational sayings. While I had great intentions, I never looked back through any of these magazines again—they were simply taking up space.

When you buy a magazine, set some ground rules. Look through it, ripping out any pages you like. Designate different notebooks for recipes, home improvements, gifts to give or favorite sayings. Place your favorites in a notebook and put the magazine in the recycle bin.

Magazines take up space in your home and in your mind. By clearing them out right away, it is one less thing you will have to worry about.

22

Musical Chairs

• • •

Every family has that one thing that causes tension, fights and tears (okay, maybe two things). In our home it is the seating arrangement at the dinner table. Strange, I know, but it has caused a number of what I will call "not so nice encounters." There is one spot that everyone cherishes and it is a battle to get it.

I decided to make our dinner table the same as my classroom. I made a seating chart. I went to a craft store, bought three small chalkboards, drilled a hole in each corner and tied them to the backs of the chairs. I wrote each of my children's names on a blackboard. At the beginning of each month I rotate the chairs one spot—the cherished seat is shared equally by everyone.

There are many things my children still battle over, but by taking one away I have one less headache to deal with.

23

Family Adventures

● ● ●

When family members go on vacation without the kids, they inevitably come home with trinkets and gifts for everyone. These are heartfelt gestures, but in our home they inevitably end up in the donation box. This is not because they are not appreciated; it is because the trinket from the far off land has no memory to the child. Flat Stanley gives us a fun and inexpensive solution to this problem.

Every year classrooms around the country read the book *Flat Stanley,* by Jeff Brown. In it, Flat Stanley gets flattened by a bulletin board and begins traveling the world through the mail. After reading the book, students get to create their own Flat Stanley and send him on an adventure. They choose a family member or friend who live somewhere exciting, color Flat Stanley, cut him out and send him off to the chosen destination. The family members or friends take pictures of Flat Stanley in their cities, write about their adventures with him and send pictures and letters back to the school. The kids sit with anticipation and excitement waiting to see where Flat Stanley went, what he saw and what he did.

Buy a journal and ask your family and friends to participate in your "Family Adventures Book." When Grandma Genevieve and Grandpa Mark go to Spain, have them take the journal. When Gigi and Papa go to New York, have them take the journal. When cousins Mylie, Molly and Will head to Canada, have them take the journal. All they need to do is write about their trip and add a few pictures. It will take less time than searching for the perfect trinket, it will save money and you will keep your home trinket-free.

As the years go by, trinkets will come and go but stories and pictures will last a lifetime. Your children will have memories of their loved ones traveling throughout the world for the rest of their lives.

Expectations

• • •

24

The Magic Wand

• • •

When my nephew was four, he was playing in one of his first t-ball games. All the parents were on the field yelling directions to their kids, trying to teach them how to play. At one point the ball landed in my nephew's glove and his dad started yelling at him, "Throw it away! Throw it away!" In our adult brain it is clear that his dad meant, "Throw it back to the pitcher!" but my nephew ran off the field, found a trash can and literally "threw it away." My nephew is now 17 and I still smile when I picture him running off the field.

Kids are not born knowing the rules of the game, the rules of life or what is expected of them—they need to be taught. When I was teaching, parents were amazed that I could simply tell my students, "cleanup" and they would. It was as if I had cast a spell with a magic wand. Believe it or not there was no magic, just lots of planning and preparation.

In your home you must teach your children what you expect from them. Begin by introducing a rule and then practice, practice, practice. Let's use clearing plates from the dinner table as an example.

Tell your kids what you expect, "When you have been excused from the table you need to take your plate to the kitchen and place it in the sink." Explain to them why this is an expectation, "Can you imagine if nobody cleared their plates? We would have a very messy house and a very tired mommy and daddy. Part of being in this family is taking care of our home. We expect you to clear your plate every night." Last but not least, model the behavior. Sit down at the table and practice until they understand what is expected. To reinforce this you can use star charts and if they choose not to cooperate they will receive a consequence. Both of these ideas will be discussed in the next two Dots.

Remember that kids are not pre-programmed with all life's rules. Teach them what you expect, hold them accountable and these expectations will become part of their daily routine. You will feel like you waved a magic wand.

25

Star Charts

• • •

Tasks are mastered through learned steps. For example, when you are learning to serve a tennis ball you throw the ball in the air, bend your other arm back and follow through to hit the ball. After continual practice these steps fade away and serving a ball simply becomes habit.

While I am not comparing our children to a tennis serve, I am saying that we need to teach our children the steps of what we expect so the action becomes habit. This is when parents can use "Star Charts." Teach a task, explain the steps and when they accomplish these steps give them a star to put on a "Star Chart." For example, when a two year old is learning to get dressed, teach him to put on his shirt, underwear and shorts. If he does this all by himself he gets a star for his chart.

Do not use "Star Charts" to reward good behavior. Choosing good behavior is expected and choosing bad behavior has consequences—

"Star Charts" are simply used to teach new tasks. Once the task is learned, the "Star Chart" goes away and one more task has been mastered.

26

Consequence Cards

• • •

How many times have you been in the heat of the moment with your child and become so angry that you ground him for life? Or even worse, you give him a consequence that inevitably punishes you. We have all been in that situation, so being prepared ahead of time takes the pressure off and keeps you from giving consequences that are completely ridiculous.

For toddlers, it is important to talk them through situations, redirect bad behavior and remove them when they are out of control. As they get older, consequence cards are helpful. Grab a pile of note cards and write different jobs that your child can do around the house: clean the windows, do his laundry, clean the toilets, weed the garden, etc. Make the cards age appropriate and even have different cards for different children. When a child receives a consequence, have him pull a card. If your child fights you on it, have him pull another card. If this becomes an issue, send him to sit in his room until he is ready to face his consequences.

Once your child has completed the consequence card, he is off the hook. If the action is something that needs further discussion, you can regain your composure while he is completing his consequence.

If you feel you need more than consequence cards, Matthew A. Johnson introduces a program to deal with consequences as well as rewards in his book, *Parenting with a Plan*. Read his book and enjoy an (almost) stress free house.

27

Open Your Mouth and
Start a Ping-Pong Match

• • •

When I was a first year teacher I spent a lot of time rethinking the mistakes I made. Now as a parent I find myself doing the same. As I tell my kids, mistakes are important as long as we choose to learn from them. An easy mistake to make as a teacher and as a parent is getting sucked into the drama. Kids know how to push buttons and I find myself saying things that I regret later.

When a child says something that makes a parent angry, the parent's first reaction is to talk back or defend himself. The moment a parent does this he has put himself into a ping-pong match with a very challenging opponent. The game goes back and forth, back and forth, but in this game no one wins.

If a parent chooses to stay calm and not respond, the game never begins and the situation is diffused. This can be so difficult. We are human and when someone is verbally attacking us, our defenses go up. Walk away, take your own time-out but don't get into a verbal match.

There is nothing worse than saying something that you will regret later. Take a moment to pause, regain your composure and then discuss what happened.

Are there times that you need to talk right away? Absolutely, but most of the time you will find this technique helpful. Should your child be held responsible for what he said to you? Definitely. Follow through with a consequence so he understands that the choice he made was wrong, but let the situation diffuse before you start handing out consequences.

28

A Place for Everything &
Everything in Its Place

• • •

When you walk into most elementary classrooms, everything has a place: backpacks hang on hooks, lunches are put in bins and homework from the night before has a special spot. This should be the same in your home. You should have a place for backpacks, a place for lunchboxes and a place for shoes. In our home backpacks are hung on hooks, lunchboxes are emptied and put in a basket and shoes are placed in a big bin by the back door. This might look different in your home, backpacks might be stacked on a shelf, lunchboxes might go in the pantry and shoes might go in a closet. Whatever works for you is fine, but all three must have a home. Make it clear to your children where these spots are. They are responsible for getting everything in the right place.

One of our goals as parents should be to teach our children responsibility. Too many times moms end up doing everything for everybody and nothing is learned. If our sons and daughters watch mom doing everything for them, they will grow up and these same sons will expect their wives to do everything for them and these same daughters will think they are expected to do everything for their family. It is a cycle that won't end unless you choose to stop it.

When morning rolls around and your child can't find his backpack, lunchbox or shoes, guess who he has to blame? Himself. It is out of your hands; it is his responsibility.

29

Mount St. Laundry

● ● ●

Mount St. Laundry is what I like to call the dirty clothes in our home. By the time I collect it, separate it, wash it, fold it and deliver it, it is time to start again.

There is an easier way. Buy a long, flat, stackable container for each member of your family and a large basket for your laundry room. Announce to your children that it is laundry day. If they want their laundry cleaned they need to bring their dirty clothes to the laundry room. Place the large basket in the laundry room and have your kids place their dirty clothes in this basket. If they choose not to, their laundry does not get cleaned. When someone says, "Mom my jersey is dirty!" I say, "Not my responsibility!" They will learn to bring their laundry the next time.

Now, it is time to begin washing. After I dry a load of clothes, I lay out my stackable containers. Put them by your dryer, take a piece of clothing out, fold it and put it into the correct container. Once all the clothes are folded the containers are ready for delivery. Have each child put his clothes away and return the container to the laundry room when he is finished. The laundry is complete and ready for the next time.

While I can't magically take your laundry away, these steps will help make it less stressful on you while teaching responsibility to your children. You have just conquered Mount St. Laundry!

30

Red Table Pick Up

• • •

I will be honest, I am a neaty—no, not needy—but neaty. I like my life neat and organized. For whatever reason my brain works better when my house is in order. One thing that has made me crazy since becoming a parent is the constant "stuff" I find all around the house. If I didn't physically stop myself I would be picking up all day long.

In the world of parenting, extremes can cause a few problems. If you are a neat freak like me you might raise neurotic children who feel controlled; if you are a dust devil mom who has dirty clothes in places like the kitchen sink or half-eaten sandwiches lurking under the couch, you might raise chaotic children; and if you are somewhere in between you are in a good spot.

Because I am really trying not to raise neurotic children, I came up with a little idea that I call "Red Table Pick Up." I have a large basket and when I feel like the "stuff" is taking over the house, I hand it to one of my children. He walks around filling the basket with dirty socks, pieces of puzzles, stuffed animals, etc. This process should take from five to ten minutes. Then he dumps everything out on our red coffee table. I make an announcement to everyone that it is "Red Table Pick Up" and anything left after ten minutes will be donated. I set the timer and it is up to them to take care of their things.

You would be amazed how quickly everything gets put away. Here is the kicker—you must be prepared to donate what is left. Children learn responsibility if there is consistency and follow through given in a loving and caring way.

31

The Kitchen is Closed

● ● ●

Do you feel like your children are grazing through the day? Do you feel like you run a restaurant all day long? Do you feel like you sit down to eat and your children aren't hungry? Are you fixing different meals for everyone? In years past, children ate breakfast, lunch and dinner, as well as a healthy after school snack. If they chose not to eat, mom didn't get up from the dinner table to fix them a quesadilla, macaroni and cheese or a peanut butter and jelly sandwich. Our generation has taken the food pendulum and swung it from one extreme to the other—we have way too many food choices.

Just like a restaurant, your kitchen can be open or closed. Get a blackboard or a switching sign and post when your kitchen is open or closed. Just because the food is there, does not mean you need to be cooking it or they need to be eating it. I always love the comment, "But mom I am starved." No! Children in different parts of the world are starved—you are hungry. Fix breakfast and then close the kitchen. Eat lunch and then close the kitchen. Make a healthy afternoon snack and then close the kitchen. Serve dinner and then close the kitchen.

Does this mean they are never going to grab a snack? No, but feeding your family should not be an all day job for you. If you plan your meals well, your children should have enough nutrients to get them through the day.

32

Dollars for Towels

• • •

As the summer months approach, my kids jump in the pool, swim for a while and run into a hot shower to warm their little bodies. In this process they change from one outfit, into a suit, dry off with a towel, use another towel getting out of the shower and put on a new outfit—with three kids this entire process gets out of control quickly. Without a plan, every piece of clothing and towel ends up on the floor or in the hamper. In no time, my children magically create an entire load of wash.

Kids don't understand that when we do the laundry money is spent on water, electricity and soap—not to mention the time it takes. This needs to be explained to kids. Tell them that you are going to charge them one dollar for any clothes or towels you find laying on the floor or any clean clothes or clean towels you find at the bottom of the hamper. Designate a jar for the money and place it in the laundry room. Explain that any money placed in the jar will help pay for water, electricity and soap.

You will most likely not collect much money. By simply explaining "why" the problem usually takes care of itself.

33

Homework Helper

• • •

Homework. It made me crazy as a teacher and it makes me insane as a parent: different grade levels, different projects, math questions that can go right over my adult brain, reading logs, math fact practice, spelling words to review, all to be managed with different personalities. It is a nightmare and a reality all at the same time. Just like everything else, make a plan.

I know it seems like a great idea to come home and give your kids some down time before homework starts, but this can backfire. Kids get tired and very cranky when you ask them to start homework after they have been lounging on the couch for an hour, playing with their favorite toy or running around in the backyard.

Try starting homework right away. Make it clear that homework must be done before any technology or outside play can take place. The faster they begin their work, the faster they get free time. While your kids do their homework, you have a job as well; go through take-home folders, empty lunch boxes and make snacks to fill their after school cravings. At the same time, answer any questions your kids have about their homework. It is a busy time, but if we don't check it off our list right away, it lingers.

Once everyone's homework is done they can enjoy some television time, arts and crafts or whatever they choose to do. Surprisingly, I find that when done first, the calm time of homework and snack has given them the rest they need and they are ready to go outside and play.

Don't think of homework as busy, miserable work. Think of it as a lesson for your children in time management—get your work done first, then there is time to play.

34

Manners Matter

● ● ●

Children who have good social skills tend to do better in general than children who do not. In other words, manners are important. Our children are not born knowing how to say "please" and "thank you," they must be taught.

Each week introduce a new social skill. There are many wonderful books available about manners. You can do an Internet search or use your own ideas to decide what you will teach your children. Next, type or write the manner of the week on a piece of paper, discuss it with your children, post it on a wall and after the week is over place it in a notebook to save. If time goes by and your children need a refresher, you have all your manners handy in your manners notebook.

When you see your child using his manners compliment him. If he forgets to use his manners remind him. Make manners a family expectation—it will help your children in the long run.

35

Even and Odd

● ● ●

When I was teaching, every student had a job. There was a line leader, a calendar helper, a paper-passer-outer and the favorite job, pencil sharpener. Things ran smoothly because everyone knew who was responsible for which job. So when my first two children spent a lot of their time arguing because they wanted to sit by the faucet in the tub, they wanted to pick the songs in the car or they wanted to get the first cookie, I thought I was going to lose my mind.

A counselor gave me some advice that literally saved my children from a mom who was one step from the loony bin. She said, "Give them each a day that they are in charge." That is when even and odd took on a whole new meaning in our home. On the odd days of the month my son was the "chooser" and on even days of the month my daughter was the "chooser." Every month we switched who was even and who was odd.

If you have more than one child, get creative: Monday and Wednesday are Morgan's days, Tuesday and Thursday are Gavin's days and Friday and Saturday are Shay's days. It doesn't matter what your plan is, as long as there is one. You will no longer be the bad guy; your children must learn to cooperate.

36

The Slumber Party Monster

• • •

Every so often a monster comes into my home, steals my child's brain and keeps it for at least one day. This is a monster that comes only once in a while and I call it the "Slumber Party Monster." Children walk into a slumber party relatively normal and by the time parents pick them up the next morning their brains are slowly being overtaken. This monster robs our children of their sanity and makes them incapable of handling the smallest problems. The only way to get our children back is through a good nap or an early bedtime the next night.

In all seriousness, lack of sleep sets our kids up for failure. In the book, *Nurture Shock: New Thinking About Children*, Po Bronson and Ashley Merryman discuss how lack of sleep can affect academic performance, emotional stability, obesity and even ADHD. They claim that some scientists believe chronic sleep deprivation can permanently change brain structure. Therefore, if you do not have a bedtime routine it is time to set one up.

First, have a bedtime board and on it list bedtime expectations: pajamas on, teeth brushed, use the potty and pick out a book. Your list might be different than mine but routine and familiarity are the key.

Second, everyone has a set time for getting in bed and a set time for lights out. In our house our youngest gets in bed first and then down the line.

Third, make it fun. Get a clipboard and make a "bedtime checklist." When Clara and Manuela are in bed go down the list; Pajamas on? Check. Teeth brushed? Check. Used the Potty? Check. In bed with book? Check. The fun of this might be enough, but if not, make a star chart.

Last but not least, read for a little while before lights out. It is a great way to calm children down before bedtime. Sweet dreams.

37

The Marshmallow Experiment

● ● ●

I always love when my kids ask me for a play-date RIGHT NOW, or they want to go to a movie RIGHT NOW or they want to go to the toy store RIGHT NOW. Let me rephrase my sarcasm—I do not love it—it drives me crazy. Children today are lacking in impulse control and delayed gratification. We live in a world of texting, instant messaging and fast food, so why wouldn't kids want it now? It is all they know.

Back in the sixties there was a research study done on impulse control and delayed gratification. It is known as the "Marshmallow Experiment." Children were told they could have one marshmallow but if they waited twenty minutes they could have two marshmallows. The children would sit in a room by themselves with one marshmallow on their plate. Some children could not wait and gobbled up the one, while others sat patiently and waited to have two. These children were tracked over the years. The children who were able to wait for two marshmallows scored higher on tests, did better in school and surpassed the other children in many ways. In other words, impulse control and delayed gratification are important life skills.

One way to work on impulse control and delayed gratification is by designating different activities for different days. If your child is always asking for play-dates at the drop of a hat, make Friday "play-date day." When he asks for a play-date with Timmy, remind him that Friday is "play-date day" and you will call his mother to plan it. If he throws a fit because he wants it NOW, tell him that nothing will be planned if that is how he chooses to act. Another example is "movie night." If your children are always asking to watch movies, make one night a week "movie night." Rent the movie, buy the popcorn and enjoy your night.

Whatever your children harass you about, give it a day and leave it at that. This will make your life easier, as well as teach your children the art of waiting.

38

I Want It Now!

• • •

As children reach the age of two, parents start to see their sweet little angels testing the system. Why can't I have anything I want in the candy aisle? Why can't I have the doughnut right now? Why can't I squirt ketchup on the carpet? This is when parenting becomes challenging and our patience is drained.

The first step is understanding that temper tantrums are expected at this age. The second step is learning how to handle them. When I was teaching and a child lost control, he was sent to the principal's office to calm down. Why? Because it was not fair to the other twenty-some students to listen as one child screamed and yelled. It also taught my students that they would not get attention for negative behavior.

This should be the same for our children. When they throw a temper tantrum, remove them from the situation. So often we hear moms say, "I just ignore them and sooner or later they stop." The only problem is while junior sits wailing uncontrollably, everyone else suffers.

Calmly remove the child from the situation. Explain that when he calms down he can return to his activity. This teaches children how to act in social situations and it shows the rest of the family that you respect them as well.

39

Role Models

• • •

Have you ever watched a child talk to a doll or a stuffed animal? He quickly becomes the parent telling his furry friend how everything should be done, "Now, you sit here and I will bring you your food. When you are finished please put your plate where it belongs." This is a child's way of reenacting what he has been taught and processing what he should be doing.

Try using this to your advantage. Bring a doll or stuffed animal with you to the store, to a restaurant, anywhere your child can model good behavior or learn good behavior. If your child is getting squirrely in his seat, comment on how nicely Bonnie Bear is sitting. If your child is sitting nicely at a restaurant tell Bonnie Bear how nice Alex is sitting. It can work both ways. It is a positive way to reinforce good behavior and your children will not even know what you are doing.

40

Restaurant Relief

● ● ●

Moms sometimes have these glorious expectations that their children will never throw a temper tantrum and when they do moms are devastated. Children are born completely self-absorbed. It is all about them and in the first few years it should be. As they grow we start putting limits on what they can and can't do and they don't like that. It is our job to teach our children these limits so as they get older the temper tantrums begin to taper off.

One place that temper tantrums seem to be inevitable is in restaurants. We take our kids to restaurants when they are hungry, they have little to no attention span and we immediately give them a sugary drink. By the time dinner comes they are screaming and won't eat. So why would we put ourselves through this kind of torture? To teach our children how we expect them to act in a restaurant.

Designate a restaurant bag and stock it with Cheerios© or some fruit, tape, paper, crayons and a stuffed animal. When you are in the car remind your child of how you expect him to act at the dinner table.

When you sit down order water or milk and give your child a few Cheerios© or cut up pieces of fruit. Children's menus are not always the healthiest, so a little nutrition to pass the time is okay. Tape a piece of paper to the table and give your child a crayon. Let him draw, doodle and scribble until his food arrives. Use the stuffed animal for role-playing good behavior.

If your child acts up, ask him to show restaurant bear how to act at the dinner table. If his behavior escalates to a temper tantrum, take him to the car and keep him there until he calms down. If he calms down you can go back inside the restaurant, but if not, stay as long as it takes. This is when cell phones are so wonderful. Call whomever is inside the restaurant and have your meal packed to take home.

If your child is older than two or three and still throws temper tantrums in restaurants, runs around and just doesn't listen, it is not too late to teach him the proper way to act. Be very clear about what you expect and if he chooses not to follow your directions, be prepared to follow through with a consequence. Often times we hand our child a technological device to pass the time. This helps in the moment, but doesn't teach a child the skills needed to interact in a social situation. Teach your child how you expect him to act in a restaurant and hold him accountable—it will help everyone in the long run.

41

The Market Meltdown

● ● ●

Anyone doing child research should sit at the Starbucks inside Target and watch the checkout line. It is the same scene you might see in a line at Disney World, but not to the same extreme. We all have had those moments when we are in a store and our child throws a tsunami of a temper tantrum. At that moment, we wish we had the power to wiggle our nose like Samantha in *Bewitched* or click our heels like Dorothy in the *Wizard of Oz*—anything to disappear. Usually we are stuck having to pull out our best parenting skills when all we want to do is join our screaming child. It is inevitable that on those occasions—and I have had my fair share—I brought my child to a store and I was unprepared.

It is easy to forget that young children have an attention span the size of a gnat and most older children think shopping is simply boring. This is when you need a bag of tricks to help make shopping a fun, learning experience.

For young children, make a shopping list using pictures from food containers or magazines. For example, cut out a picture of eggs, a milk container or strawberries. Tape them on a paper and give the list to your child, putting him in charge of finding the items. Play *I-Spy* while walking down the aisles, "I see something red. I see something yummy to eat." Make up silly songs about the item you are looking for and have your child guess what it is.

For older children, make lists of things they need to find and turn it into a scavenger hunt. Challenge them to find the least expensive items on their list or the food with the least amount of sugar. Finally, have them guess the total cost.

Being prepared and involving children in the process of shopping teaches them many life lessons. The best part is your child will not be screaming and yelling in the middle of the produce aisle.

42

What If Everyone Did It?

● ● ●

What if everyone did it? This is a question I use constantly during the day. When my youngest doesn't want to clean up her toys, I say, "What if everyone left their toys on the ground?" When one of my children drops a gum wrapper on the ground, I say, "What if everyone left their gum wrappers on the ground?" When everyone leaves their plates sitting at the dinner table, I say, "What if we left our dirty plates at the table every day?" The answer is we would have a messy house and a messy world. This simple question helps our children understand that we are not nagging them, but teaching them to be responsible for their place in this world.

43

That's Not Fair!

• • •

"That's not fair! She got to go to the zoo and I didn't!" How many times have you heard the "unfair" comment and either became really frustrated, felt really guilty or maybe a little of both? The reality is life can be unfair. The opening line of M. Scott Peck's book, *The Road Less Travelled*, is "Life is difficult." If we teach kids that life is not always going to go their way and that sometimes life is unfair or difficult, they will not be so shocked and overwhelmed when it doesn't go their way.

When you get the "unfair" comment stay calm and simply explain that sometimes Tony gets to go on a special day with grandma and sometimes Sam gets to go. Sometimes Maddy gets a new outfit for school and sometimes Abby does. Sometimes mommy drives on Ben's field trip and sometimes mommy drives on Hank's. It is not a competition, it is real life.

We as parents can make ourselves insane trying to balance everything for our kids. Make life easier on yourself as well as your children. The more we teach them about the realities of life today, the happier and better adjusted they will be in the future.

44

Two Ears, One Mouth

● ● ●

I believe we have two ears and one mouth for one reason, to listen more and talk less. How many times have you been in a "one-way" conversation with your child? He talks and talks and talks or even yells and yells and yells, and nothing gets accomplished? I have been in this situation more times than I care to admit. That is until I decided to teach my kids how to have "real" conversations.

A "real" conversation is when two people interact, verbally sharing ideas, opinions or feelings—listening and speaking goes back and forth and back and forth, like throwing a ball. Can you imagine going to play catch with your child and every time he threw it to you, you purposely dropped it? Your child would get frustrated and the game would be over. This is the same with a conversation. If one person is doing all the talking and no listening, the conversation needs to be over. Tell your child that when he is willing to speak AND listen the conversation can begin again. Until then, walk away.

It is so hard to truly focus on listening to others, but it is such an important lesson in life. Teach your children the skills involved in listening. Can you imagine if everyone really started listening? What a different world it would be.

45

The Dog Ate My Homework

• • •

Quick question, quick answer—
Your child left his homework at home. What do you do?

    (a) become so angry you stew about it all day
    (b) quickly run his homework to school
    (c) let natural consequences take effect

If you answered (a) or (b) read on. If you answered (c), you are on the right track and you can stop reading here.

It is time to be honest with yourself and ask the question why? Let's start with (a). Children make mistakes and they should. It is how they learn. The problem is how parents handle these mistakes. If we are always expecting nothing but perfection children will stop trying for fear of failure.

Let's look at (b). Children will never learn to deal with failure if parents are fixing everything for them. We as parents spend way too much time cushioning our children from their own mistakes and therefore we raise children who cannot handle the real world.

Natural consequences are the best way for our children to learn. So let's look at this question again. Your child left his homework at home. What do you do? For the moment you do nothing. You don't freak out and you don't take it to him. You let natural consequences fall into place. Will his grade drop? Maybe. Will he be embarrassed? Maybe. Will he be sad or angry? Maybe. Will he forget his homework again? Most likely not.

Turn your child's mistakes into learning experiences. Remind yourself that you are his teacher, his coach and his guide. You are not his enemy or his savior. Take a step back and allow for natural consequences to take place. He might not thank you now, but when he can handle disappointments in the future you can quietly thank yourself.

46

I Am Not an Octopus

• • •

I am not an octopus, but my children think I am. While having eight arms would be magnificent, I believe parents have only two for a reason. If we do everything for our children it deprives them of learning to be responsible and independent. I believe my children are very capable of getting a glass of water by themselves, yet it is inevitable that while I have twenty things going on at one time, someone asks me for a glass of water.

Sit everyone down and tell them it is time for a show. Explain that they will be acting in, "I Am Not an Octopus." Place one child up front and continue to put things in his arms until nothing more fits. When he reaches his capacity and is dropping things all over the floor, explain that this is how mom feels when everyone is asking for things at one time. The kids will giggle, but they will understand. The next time they ask you to do something that they are capable of doing themselves, all you have to say is, "I am not an octopus."

47

No More Nagging Mommy

• • •

I don't know about you, but I get very tired repeating the same thing over and over: "Did you clean your room? Did you clean your room? Did you clean your room?" The broken record thing makes me very cranky and not so nice.

As a teacher, I always wrote what I expected of my students on the board: write your name on the back of the paper; draw a picture of yourself on the other side; put your picture in the assignment basket; and take out a book to read when you are done. They knew what to do. If they got off task I simply reminded them to read the list on the board. I would go about my business and I was not the "nagging teacher." If my students did not finish their work, they would stay inside at recess. I never raised my voice or got mad; by writing my expectations down it became their responsibility, not mine.

This works in your home as well. Designate a place for writing and mark down what you expect your kids to do. A while back it was my mom's birthday and we were going to her home to celebrate. I needed my kids to clean their rooms, get showered, dressed and make a card for her. I wrote down all four things and went to get ready myself. It was out of my hands and into theirs. They knew what was expected and they checked it off the list when they were done. Will it always go smoothly? No, but it begins teaching them to be responsible for themselves and the "nagging mommy" goes away.

48

What Are We Doing Today?

• • •

When I was teaching the schedule was written on the board every-day and my students knew exactly what to expect. One day I arrived at school late and forgot to write the daily schedule on the board. I was shocked at how many kids became anxious not knowing what the day entailed.

Jill Stamm discusses the important correlation between consistent routines and a child's security and behavior in her book, *Bright from the Start*. In other words, when a child knows what to expect he feels more secure and behaves better.

Therefore, have consistent routines in your home and let your children know what to expect each day. By doing this, Stamm says you are providing a "sense of security the brain needs to develop properly." By giving our children a routine we are making our own lives easier; we are making our children's lives easier; and we are helping our child's brain to develop properly—a win, win, win situation. It doesn't get much better than that.

Feelings

• • •

49

You Are the Best

• • •

We have become a nation of praise, but if praise is not specific it can be harmful. Have you ever told your child that he is so smart, he is so talented or he is the best athlete? While parents have the best intentions, giving children general praise can actually hurt rather than help.

In Carol S. Dweck's book, *Mindset*, Dweck discusses the difference between the fixed mindset and the growth mindset. Someone with a fixed mindset believes that his qualities are fixed from birth and they can't be changed. Someone with the growth mindset believes that qualities are things that can be cultivated through hard work. The most successful humans, Dweck believes, are those who have a growth mindset.

When a child receives general praise he will have a fixed mindset. A child with this frame of mind will eventually give up trying because he fears he will not be able to live up to his potential. An example of general praise would be, "What are you nervous about? You have so much natural ability. No one is better than you."

When a child receives specific praise he will have a growth mindset. A child with this frame of mind will keep challenging himself to do and be better because he feels that he has control over his talent. The harder I work, the better I will become. An example of specific praise is, "You did well because you worked hard. You never gave up. You kept on trying."

Always try to praise for specific effort versus general praise. Your children will internalize the importance of trying their hardest instead of giving up for fear that they cannot live up to the expectations.

50

Things Are Not Always as They Seem

• • •

Sometimes the best advice comes right from our children. A while back our family was having a discussion about a child who was being mean. I began going into my mommy lecture on what to do and my daughter said simply, "When someone is mean on the outside, maybe something is hurting on the inside." Wow! She nailed it on the head.

This is something we should remember about our own children as well. It is easy to come down on a child for being mean to his sibling without understanding why he is doing it in the first place. These are the moments that we need to read between the lines. First and foremost, a child needs to take responsibility for hurting others, but then take the time to figure out if something is hurting him on the inside. It might be as easy as a little one-on-one time and sometimes it might take more help than that. Either way, remember things are not always as they seem.

51

Disappointed vs. Sad

• • •

How many times have your children fallen apart because they didn't get to go on that play-date they were hoping for; they didn't get to see the movie they wanted; or they didn't get to eat at the restaurant they picked? I try my hardest not to scream to the universe, "Are you kidding, there are children starving in our world and you are upset by this?" My child's eyes fill with tears and he says, "but mom you don't understand, I am just sad!" My anger quickly turns to guilt. How could I possibly be such an insensitive mother? I am not allowing my child to feel his emotions.

This is when we as moms need to put on the brakes. Yes, it is important to teach our children to be in touch with their emotions, but as moms today have moved more into the corner of, "you must feel and express everything," our children are losing sight of reality.

Discuss the difference between being disappointed and being sad. We are sad when we are hurt or a friend is hurt, when someone dies, when a classmate is bullying us. We are disappointed when we don't get to go on a play-date, go to the movies or pick out the restaurant we want. When our child is sad we are there to hold him, to cry with him, to feel with him. When he is disappointed we are there to say, "Life is unfair sometimes. I am sorry you are disappointed." Then we move on.

At first this might seem insensitive, but if our children don't learn to deal with disappointments they will lose out on a skill that will affect every aspect of their lives. Remind your children of the difference between disappointed and sad and they will become more aware of their reactions to life.

52

Look Who Is Talking

● ● ●

Let's say that your child is in 1st grade and the teacher is presenting a lesson on dinosaurs. She is leading a discussion on how big dinosaurs really were. The children are enthralled and then a cell phone rings. The teacher walks to her desk, answers the phone and proceeds to have a ten minute conversation, gossiping with a friend. As time goes by, the children become a little stir crazy. Some kids begin running around the classroom, others get things out that they shouldn't. A handful of students try talking to the teacher. The teacher hangs up the phone and yells at everyone for their behavior. She tells them they have been disrespectful and takes away their recess. After regaining her composure, she picks up where she left off.

Five minutes into the lesson the phone rings again. She proceeds to answer it and this time talks for fifteen minutes. Once again, the kids in the classroom slowly go from a quiet hum to a load roar. When the teacher gets off the phone she screams, "YOU ARE ALL IN BIG TROUBLE! YOU HAVE NOT ONLY LOST YOUR MORNING RECESS,

BUT ALSO YOUR AFTERNOON RECESS! PUT YOUR HEADS ON YOUR DESKS AND DO NOT TALK!"

How would you feel if this was your child's teacher? What would you do? Would you discuss this with the teacher? Call the principal? Complain to friends? I would be really frustrated with the teacher's actions, but this is what I do in my own home. I sit down to play a board game, read or do a craft with my children and the phone rings. I answer it and talk as long as I want. If my children bother me or get loud and crazy, I become unglued.

Children need to learn respect and have manners when their parents are on the phone, but parents also need to be respectful of one-on-one time with their children. Set a timer, sit and play with your child and do not answer the phone, send a text or check emails during that time. Let him know that your time together is important. Once time is up, explain to your child that you need to get some work done. He will be much more forgiving knowing that you just gave him quality time. Giving children undivided attention can make all the difference in the world.

53

Walkie Talkies

• • •

I am not talking about the little hand held devices that my kids absolutely adore. I am talking about walking and talking. With three children, two dogs, a hamster, five frogs and too many fish to count life gets insane! At least ten times a day I find myself doing things that make no sense: handing my son the princess costume my daughter wanted; putting my keys in the refrigerator; or walking back to my bedroom with no recollection of what I was getting or doing. Sound familiar? It is so easy to get lost in the craziness of the day that we miss those moments of one-on-one time with each child.

Our family was going through a stressful time a while back and it seemed like no one was getting along. I decided to begin taking each child, by himself, on a walk once a week. Whenever something went wrong during the week and there was no time to talk about it I would say, "Let's make sure we remember to talk about this on our walk" and we would. Those walks made a huge difference. Each child got some time with mom and they all felt validated.

It does not matter whether you walk, grab a bite to eat or sit in your backyard, as long as it is planned with no interruptions your children will appreciate the time. They might not say it, but I guarantee you will see it in their actions.

54

Do What Is Right For Your Child

• • •

This might sound like a strange title because it seems unimaginable that we wouldn't do what was right for our children, but sometimes we make choices based on comfort rather than what is right. Our children need to see just the opposite.

I can remember being at a park with my kids and some other families we knew. One of the children was bullying everyone—saying mean things, not taking turns and pushing and shoving other kids. I didn't know the mom well, so I was uncomfortable saying anything to her. When my kids came to me for help I would say, "Just go play somewhere else. It's not a big deal." But it was a big deal to my kids and I wasn't helping. I was concerned I would hurt the other mom's feelings. In that moment I put someone else's feelings in front of my children's feelings.

Not too long after, one of the other moms confronted the child and confronted the mom. The mom was apologetic, the child was put in time-out and I learned a valuable lesson in that moment—do what is right for your children.

By choosing to do what is right for our children, we teach them that their feelings are important. Children need to know that if they cannot protect themselves, we are there to help. By giving them this gift, they will feel secure. Feeling secure gives them self-esteem to solve their own problems. Solving problems gives them confidence. And confidence is one of the greatest gifts our children can earn.

55

Watch What You Say

• • •

Have you ever been in a situation when your child runs to his room in tears and you have no idea why? Like when your daughter sobs uncontrollably because you told the neighbor that your daughter thought her son was very nice. In your adult brain making this comment is a way to let the other mom know that she has a nice son—to your daughter it is the end of her world.

As a teacher, I had a rule when talking with parents about their children, my students were not allowed to listen to our conversations. Children were not allowed at conferences and notes sent home were sealed in an envelope. I also made sure to keep my private conversations with colleagues, friends and parents away from my students. Adult talk is just that, adult talk.

Pay attention to what you are saying in front of your children. Our children are more aware than you realize and something that might seem harmless to you could be horribly devastating to them. If we want to teach our children respect, it starts with the way we treat them.

56

Meat in the Middle

● ● ●

Since the day our third child was born I began calling our middle child, "Our Meat in the Middle." I explained that a sandwich has a piece of bread, a stack of meat, followed by another piece of bread. Bread is yummy on its own, but without the meat there is no sandwich. Our family is a "sandwich" and without our middle daughter our family is not complete.

Being the middle child might seem challenging, but in Kevin Leman's book, *The Birth Order Book: Why You Are the Way You Are*, Leman states that being a middle child might not be as bad as it seems. The middle child can sometimes feel ignored or left out, but in the end being in the middle forces him to find his own way. If your middle child knows he fills a special spot in the family, he will find comfort during the challenging times and become stronger because of it.

57

What's Going On?

• • •

Have you ever had someone say that you looked tired, seemed frazzled or were really cranky? How does that make you feel? I know for me it sometimes makes me feel self-conscious, other times I am stunned and every once in a while it just makes me angry. But this is what we do to our children all the time.

While getting in touch with feelings is a good thing, interpreting those feelings for our children can put them on the defensive. Instead of saying, "Wow, you sure seem angry" or "You are acting really jealous of your little sister right now," try simply asking them, "What is going on?"

Not too long ago I began paying close attention to how I confront my children and was surprised at how much I was interpreting their feelings. One of my children was really upset about something. Normally I would say, "You seem to be in meltdown mode. You must not have gotten enough sleep last night because you are so angry!" This would infuriate my child and she would scream back, "I am not tired or angry. You are so mean!" In a matter of seconds I had started a fight that completely got away from dealing with her feelings and made it about me. On this specific occasion I did not interpret what I saw, I simply said, "What's going on?" My child turned to me, started crying in my arms and said, "I am just so tired!" I could then validate her feelings and help her problem solve, "I am so sorry you are tired. Do you think it would make sense to get to bed early tonight?"

Pay attention to how you are responding to your children and their feelings. You might be surprised how a simple question such as, "What's going on?" can completely change a situation.

58
You Can't Mess Up Art

• • •

You can't mess up art because it is an expression of self. Expressing yourself is not right or wrong, it is simply who you are. While it sounds like a strange statement, it is a great lesson to teach our kids about artwork as well as life. It is easy as a parent to look at our child's creation and think it could use a little more color here or a few more circles there, but in sharing this with our child we take away from his creativity, uniqueness and expression. If we do this often, our child could become a perfectionist or give up completely. Nothing will ever be good enough.

As hard as it might be, bite your tongue and let your children create what they want, not what you want. Even if your child is drawing a stick figure and his friend is drawing a Picasso, that is okay. If he is trying his hardest, then his artwork is special to him—let it be special to you as well.

59

The Talking Stick

● ● ●

When I was teaching there were always those students who had a story to tell or a question to answer. I think they would have taught the class if I had let them. Then there were the students who hardly spoke a word. If I didn't make eye contact and physically try to interact with them, a day could go by and not a word would come out of their mouths.

In order to balance the two, I had a "Talking Stick." When a student was holding the talking stick he was talking and no one was allowed to interrupt. This helped the attention-getters to work on controlling their desire to dominate everything and allowed the wallflowers to be heard.

Try using a "Talking Stick" at the dinner table. Whether it is a spoon or something more creative, it will give each child a chance to be heard. Ask a question for everyone to answer or simply let the holder of the stick talk. It is a great lesson in impulse control for your "talkers" and a great lesson in opening up for your less talkative kids.

60

Worry Dolls and Magic Powers

• • •

I can remember being a little girl and being deathly afraid of night-time. I was scared of the dark. No matter what a child is scared of, it can create such a helpless feeling. We as parents can't take a child's fear away, but we can give him the power to help himself.

Not too long ago we were vacationing in Mexico. I came across these little baskets that I almost missed. Inside each basket were five tiny dolls each no bigger than half my pinky's fingernail. The directions read, "When you go to bed at night, tell one worry to each doll, place the dolls under your pillow and when you wake up in the morning the dolls will have taken your worries away." I bought these for my kids because I thought they were cute.

At bedtime, my youngest daughter, who was scared of the dark, began talking to her worry dolls. She told each worry doll about a fear, put them under her pillow and proceeded to fall asleep without a peep. In the morning I asked her how she slept and she said, "I slept great. I didn't need to worry about the dark because the dolls did that for me." By simply giving her fear to something else it took the stress off her.

Stanley I. Greenspan talks about four principles that help children feel secure in his book, *The Secure Child: Helping Our Children Feel Safe and Confident in a Changing World*. One of these principles is reassurance. Reassuring children that they are protected is important to feeling secure: they are protected by mom and dad, teachers, doctors, firefighters and the police. Worry dolls are another way for a child to feel protected.

Create your own worry dolls. In doing so, you are giving your children the power to handle their fears.

61

Write It Down

• • •

Writing or drawing is an amazing way to let children get out what they don't feel comfortable saying. By writing a story or drawing a picture a child can express his feelings that seem too difficult to share.

When a friend's son was in first grade his teacher was concerned with a drawing from this boy's journal. Without getting into too many details, it involved a boy, a bear, a knife and lots of blood. Needless to say the mom was concerned. In working with a counselor, they came to find out that this boy was dealing with anxiety. The counselor felt he was depicting his fear of being powerless and wanting to conquer that fear in his drawing. This picture opened up the door for a dialogue with this child, helping him understand what he was feeling.

While this is an extreme example, our children will go through emotional times and writing or drawing can be very therapeutic. Buy your child a journal or a sketchbook and give him the privacy and freedom to explore his feelings. These stories and drawings open up a conversation that might not have occurred otherwise.

62

Back and Forth

• • •

The older our kids become the less willing they seem to communicate with mom and dad. Ironically, this is when communication is so important. I can remember being a teenager and acting as if my parents' point of view was unimportant to me when deep down inside I needed their advice and acceptance more than ever.

Buy a journal to pass back and forth between you and your child. Start off writing a question, comment or concern in the journal and leave it on your child's bed.

He can respond to your question and return it to you. Back and forth the journal goes without a word being spoken. Writing is a non-intrusive way to gather insight into your child and what is going on in his life. He may act as if it is silly or stupid, but deep down he will appreciate the comfort in knowing you are there.

63

Birthday Letters

• • •

Every year, on each of my children's birthdays, I write a letter to them. In this letter I write a summary of their year: what they did for fun, their hobbies, what activities they participated in, personality traits, anything that was special to them. I do this with one purpose in mind, to remind my children what they loved to do when they were young.

When I was a young girl I was constantly organizing my things, creating small businesses and doing any arts and crafts I could get my hands on. As I grew up, life took over and I lost touch with these early loves. Now I look at my life and realize that those early days encompassed who I truly am. While it looks a little different, I am the happiest when I am organized and creating.

Each of us has a very special and individual journey that takes us in many directions. Our early years are the foundation for this journey and these letters help to remind our children of their uniqueness. Write your child a letter, place it in a notebook and give it to him when he is grown—what a special birthday gift that will last a lifetime.

64

Dinner with Mom and Dad

• • •

As funny as it might seem, when I was teaching 1st grade the students loved the reward of having lunch with me. While I would like to say it was because of my charm and wit, I know better. For a young child, having lunch with a teacher is about getting to eat somewhere other than the cafeteria, telling his friends all about it, one-on-one attention and feeling like the coolest student in the classroom—even if it is for just one lunch hour.

The same is true in your home. Take your children out for dinner one at a time with mom, dad or, better yet, both. Parents sometimes forget that they are raising individuals who need alone time with mom and dad. Let your child pick the place, dress yourselves up and enjoy the special time. Your young children will cherish the moment and your older children will appreciate the kind gesture—someday!

65

The Talk Box

• • •

When I was teaching, I had a "Talk Box." At the beginning of the
year I would explain what the box was used for:

> When you have an issue with another child please write
> it down and place it in the "Talk Box." If it is an emer-
> gency I will deal with it immediately; otherwise, we will
> schedule different times in the week to discuss what is
> in the "Talk Box."

If the kids felt a problem was very important, they would write it
down, but if it was more of a "tattle" it would inevitably fizzle. This
usually left the important questions, complaints and problems for discussion. I was not constantly in the middle of the bickering, but children felt validated when it really mattered.

Make a "Talk Box," put paper and pens next to it and explain what
your children need to do. If your children are too young to write, have

them draw a picture. Go through the notes ahead of time so you are prepared to handle whatever is in the box. This gives you time to teach your children the lessons they need without saying the wrong thing in the heat of the moment.

66

Trapped Time

• • •

The car is one of the best times to talk to your children because, unless they plan on walking home from where you are, they are trapped. For years my kids would get in the car after a play-date, camp or school and I would ask, "How was your day?" Inevitably they would respond, "Fine," and then silence. Not exactly the answer I was looking for.

I realized I was asking a dead-end question, so I became a little more creative in my approach. When my kids get in the car after school I tell them about my day. I am not putting them on the spot and they are given a little time to wind down from their day. After a while I throw out one question for everyone that is more specific, "Did anything funny happen at school?" "Did anything make you mad today?" "What was your high and low today?" "What did you learn today that you didn't know?" "Did you ask any interesting questions?" These are questions that get the conversation going and bring out feelings that might not have come to the surface otherwise.

67

Tiger Mom

• • •

Not too long ago an article was published in the *Wall Street Journal* titled, "Why Chinese Mothers are Superior." The author Amy Chua compared mothers in the west to mothers in the east. Whether you agreed with the article or not, it brought about a nation-wide debate. What I found fascinating was her comment on self-esteem. I am paraphrasing, but Chua in so many words said mothers in the west try to teach self-esteem while mothers in the east expect self-esteem.

Some parents worry that the teacher is being too hard on their child. They call and write coaches with concerns when their child isn't playing enough. Some parents believe that everyone should win and take home a ribbon. I nearly croaked a few years back when an article in the paper was talking about how teachers were going to use purple pens to grade their student's papers because red seemed too harsh on a child's self-esteem. There is a fear that if our children fail they will have low self-esteem. Ironically, this is not true. Children have low self-esteem when they don't feel confident in themselves and it is virtually impossible to feel confident if you have never learned to pick yourself up from failure.

Believe in the resiliency of your children and let them fail. Does this mean you leave them high and dry during these hard times? No. You support them, you listen to them, you love them, but ultimately you give them the power to solve their own problems.

68

Take Off Your Cape

• • •

Do you ever feel like Superwoman, flying around town trying to look perfect? The problem is that in real life we are not Superheroes, we are humans who make mistakes everyday.

A friend of mine came to me worried about her daughter. After receiving a B on her report card, her daughter was devastated. The daughter aimed for perfection in everything that she did, but when she made a mistake she felt horrible about it. She would beat herself up saying how stupid she was. This mom was heart broken. Why was her daughter so hard on herself?

The mom took her daughter to counseling and in the very first session the daughter was asked to draw a picture of her family. In the drawing the dad and siblings were dressed in normal clothes, but the mom was dressed like Superwoman. When the counselor asked why she had drawn her mom like a Superhero the daughter replied, "My mom is Supermom. She does everything right." The mom was blown away. Her response was, "That is not true, I make tons of mistakes." The counselor asked the daughter, "What does your mom do when she makes a mistake?" The daughter responded, "She gets very angry with herself."

If you are a Supermom trying to do everything for everyone and do it to perfection, remember that you have little eyes watching your every move. Make mistakes, tell your kids about them and sometimes make light of them. Take off your cape and laugh at your mistakes—your kids will not be so hard on themselves in the future.

69

You Choose

• • •

While there are many things in life that we can't control, one thing we can control is our choice. You can't control what someone does or says to you, but you can choose how you will react to it. This is such an important tool to teach children.

If I had a quarter for every time one of my children changed their mood or behavior based on a sibling interaction I would be rich: "He made me so angry I had to pinch him."; "My whole day is ruined because she colored my hamster green!"; "He made me squirt all the toothpaste in the toilet." He did this; she did that; and what did you choose to do?

Remind your kids that they are the only ones who can choose how they will react. They might become upset, angry or frustrated, but they ultimately get to decide how they will let it affect them in the long run. Are you going to let someone else pick how you feel? You decide. Remember—it's your choice.

70

Daddy's Girl

● ● ●

Girls need their daddies or a daddy figure in their lives. This is such a simple statement, but one that completely affects our daughters. In his book, *Bringing up Girls*, James Dobson lays the groundwork for why dads are so important in the lives of girls. Dobson states that, "A daughter's self-worth and confidence is linked directly to her dad." So listen up dads!

It is not unusual for families to follow same sex lines: the mom does the girl stuff and the dad does the boy stuff. The mom takes her daughter shopping, to do her nails and to volleyball lessons, while the dad takes his son to baseball practice, football games and to fix the car. This gives girls the wrong message.

Dads, take your daughter shopping, be involved in her sports teams and teach her how to fix the car. Go on bike rides with your daughter, take her to get her haircut and teach her how to throw a football. Most importantly, talk to her. Tell your daughter how precious she is to you, how much you love her and how beautiful she is on the inside and the outside.

If a daughter gets the love and attention she needs from her dad, she will not look for attention from the wrong crowd. She will expect kindness. She will expect respect. She will expect the love she deserves.

71

Mama's Boy

● ● ●

I will never forget my first day of teaching fifth grade. All the kids came in, put their backpacks on a hook and found their seats—all except for Michael. Michael's mom walked in, took his picture and then gave him a big hug and kiss as she walked out the door. Within the first two minutes of fifth grade, it was clear—Michael was going to be bullied and teased.

A mother-son relationship is a very special one, but how mothers handle it will determine a lot for their sons. Michael Gurian talks about what mothers should expect during their son's second decade of life in his book, *The Wonder of Boys: What Parents, Mentors and Educators Can Do to Shape Boys into Exceptional Men*. As boys enter this phase, it is important to give them more independence. Does this mean that you cut the umbilical cord completely? No. Let him know you are always there for him, but also let him know you respect his need for independence. When your son is grown—if you have given this gift to him—he will appreciate you and respect you for giving him the freedom to grow.

Values

● ● ●

72

A Lesson from the Garden

• • •

What happens when you take a beautiful bouquet of flowers and smash them into a vase? Within a few days you will no longer have beautiful flowers, but wilted, dead flowers. On the other hand, what happens when you take a few flowers and place them into that same vase? They last longer. When you are scheduling your life and your children's lives, think of this analogy. If you want your family to bloom and be beautiful from the inside out, don't over-schedule.

Try using this mentality when signing up for different jobs in your child's classroom. Instead of signing up for a little bit of everything and spreading yourself too thin, pick one thing to concentrate on: library volunteer, lunch volunteer, art masterpiece or pick one party to plan. Go to as many parties as you want, but instead of feeling like you should be on every committee, put your volunteer time into one.

As for your kids, keep it simple. Parents are scheduling so much for their children that they are complicating what could and should be a simple life. Ironically, studies are showing that children do better academically when they participate in unstructured, spontaneous play. I am not saying to cut out all activities, but minimizing them is important.

Look at all aspects of your life and pick and choose what you want to do. Do you want to be a family of wilted flowers or a beautiful, blooming family? It seems like an easy choice to me.

73

The Question

• • •

Moms run all over the town, while in the process they run themselves into the ground. There have been many times as a parent that I have known myself only as mom. It is in those times when I ask myself one question, "How would I feel if my daughters were leading the life I was leading?" In those moments I realize I need to find a balance between motherhood and self because my children are watching and learning from everything I do.

If you look in the mirror and ask yourself "The Question," what would you answer? Teaching children the balance between loving and caring for family as well as loving and caring for self is a very special gift.

74

A Piece of the Pie

• • •

Many moms today are doing so much for everyone else that they don't realize they are not taking care of themselves. As I tell this story I want you to think about how you would end it. There are no right or wrong answers.

It has been a very long day and you are tired. You have spent all day thinking about eating your favorite pie. You go to a restaurant and order a piece. You are just about to take your first bite when someone you care about walks in and says, "Oh that is my very favorite kind of pie! Can I please have it?"

What do you do? Like I said, there are no right or wrong answers, but it is a wonderful glimpse into how your loved ones affect you.

In years past, I probably would have given my pie to any person on the street, but my story has changed. Now I would explain to my loved one that I needed to fill myself up first. When I was filled, not stuffed, I would share what was left with them. If there was no pie left, I would help them brainstorm how they could get a piece of pie.

While to some this may sound selfish, it is not. Parents can take care of no one if they don't take care of themselves. By taking care of yourself, you can then take care of your family and in the end there will be pie for everyone. How sweet it is!

75

Fill Up Your Cup

● ● ●

I always love when people comment on how much vacation time teachers get: "Teachers have the best job in the world. They get three months off during summer, a winter break and a spring break." Yes, they do and, yes, they need it. During these breaks they inevitably end up taking classes to further their education and come back early to prepare for the school year, but ultimately they spend time doing the things they love so they are refreshed, relaxed and ready to teach our children.

A few years ago I went to a convention. In one of the seminars we were asked to write down everything we did in a day, being as specific as possible. My day started at 5:00am and ended at 11:00pm. The only thing I had done for myself was buy a Starbuck's tea and exercise at 5:30 in the morning. I don't know about you, but I am not too sure that exercising at 5:30 in the morning even counts. This was very eye opening. I was headed towards burn out and knew I needed a change, if not for myself, for my family.

I want you to try three things. First, write down everything you do in a day and see how you are treating yourself. Second, write down all the things you remember doing and loving as a child. Our early years help remind us of our true self. If you can't remember what you loved doing as a child, ask your mom, dad, older siblings or friends if they remember. It might look different as an adult, but it will give you a glimpse into your true self. Last but not least, schedule time for yourself every day. This is not time to go to the grocery store, run to the cleaners, pick up dinner, clean the house or pay the bills. This is giving yourself a little time everyday to do something you love. This might mean getting a babysitter, swapping babysitting time with a friend or simply getting up before everyone else. No matter how you find the time, you must fill your cup before you can fill everyone else's.

76

Find Yourself in a Magazine

• • •

Now that we realize the importance of filling ourselves up, it is time to figure out what that looks like. For me, I spent the first eight years of parenting floating around looking for my lost identity. I was a mom and a wife, but I was no longer myself. When I decided to pursue a Master of Arts in Professional Counseling I felt my identity slowly seep back into my body. I was only taking one class a session, but by making that simple move, I became a better mom. I had something that was just mine.

If you are floating around looking for your identity, the time has come to find it. Walk the magazine aisle of a bookstore. Look at every magazine and pick out the ones that catch your eye. You might have no idea why you picked what you did, but something within you was drawn to it. Buy the magazines and look through them. Rip out the pictures or articles that you are drawn to and glue them on a paper, pin them to a bulletin board or lay them in front of you.

Now is when you get creative. What do you see? What do you love? What are you drawn to? This is the first step in finding the piece of your identity that might be missing. Do you need to act on it right away and go full force? Not necessarily. Sometimes happiness can begin with awareness followed by baby steps. Find that missing piece, be a better parent—everyone wins.

77

The Happy List

• • •

Finding yourself in a magazine will help you find what you love doing, but happiness also comes in what we surround ourselves with every day. Your happy list will help you do just that.

Before the school year starts teachers spend up to a month preparing their classrooms. It was no different for me. The classroom was my office. I spent more time there than I did in my own home. For this reason I made sure to have things in it that made me happy.

What makes you happy? It is a simple question, but one we sometimes forget as moms. By surrounding ourselves with things that make us smile, we inevitably become happier.

It is time to make your list. These are not unrealistic things, but small things: flowers, shells, children's books, teacups, etc. Once your list is done find a way to put these things in your home. Sometimes it is the simple things in life that put a smile on our face—and if mommy is happy everyone is happy!

78

Creating Tradition

• • •

Holiday traditions are such an important part of family. It is not so much what the tradition is, but that you do the same thing every year. They are the hooks holding a family together, even after the children are raised.

Think through your family traditions. What do you do as a family? In our home I buy everyone Christmas jammies and they open them on Christmas Eve. On Thanksgiving, I create a fake tree out of twigs, place it in a pot and cut out colorful leaves to tape on the tree. On these leaves we write all the things we are thankful for. Every Halloween, we cook chili and hang donuts from the tree and the kids in the neighborhood try to eat them without using their hands. On Fourth of July, we decorate our bikes, wagons and carts and participate in a parade. For Easter, I ask the Easter bunny to hide the kids' baskets and leave clues.

Sometimes the smallest things we do every year might not seem like a tradition, but those are the things that your children will remember and carry with them. It is never too late to start up new traditions, so enjoy your old traditions and have fun creating some new ones as well.

79

Play-Date Donation

• • •

When my son was around two, we spent many days at the park. I had a group of friends who would meet once a week to let the kids play and my friends and I would get some needed adult interaction. At the same time, it seemed as if my son was constantly blowing through one stage and into the next—he was growing out of clothes, growing out of diapers, starting rice cereal, moving to solids and then moving to table foods. With each stage brought a pile of things he no longer needed.

This is when our group started "Play-Date Donation." Once a month we decided what items we would bring for donation: diapers, bottles, socks, toiletries, toys—you name it. We would then donate what we collected to a local charity. It helped clean out our homes, helped those in need and started a process of giving that I want to be a part of my children's lives forever.

80

Movie Night for Others

● ● ●

Teaching children to help others is such an important life lesson and it can also be fun. Whether it is planning a movie night, an art auction, a talent show or something else, children can take on the responsibility of planning a party from start to finish, while helping others at the same time. It is a win-win situation.

For movie nights, have your children decide whom to invite, make the invitations, pick out a movie and plan the evening. Ask the kids to wear their pajamas and bring a pillow. The price of their ticket, popcorn and drink is a donation. When the guests arrive, have a ticket booth, collect the money, distribute the snacks and enjoy the movie.

An art auction is another fun way to make money for others. Invite a group of children and their parents to the big event and ask each child to bring a few of their best pieces of artwork. On the night of the auction, charge a fee for admission or simply make your money during the auction.

Last but not least, try a talent show. Send out invitations with the rules, set up the stage, prepare the snacks and enjoy the performances. Once again, you can charge a set fee for admission or simply ask for a donation.

Get creative. You will be amazed what children come up with when given the chance. No matter what you decide, help your children plan the event from start to finish. They will not only feel great helping others, but will also feel an amazing sense of accomplishment.

81

Random Acts of Kindness

● ● ●

When my son was in preschool, his class created a "Random Acts of Kindness Chain." Whenever the teachers saw someone doing something kind, they would write it on a 2" x 11" strip of paper and place it in the "Random Acts of Kindness Box." If the students saw someone doing something kind, they could do the same with a little help from the teachers. At the end of the week, the teachers would read through each strip of paper and staple them onto the chain. The class talked about how long the chain was becoming and how all the links represented one happy moment that multiplied into more happy moments.

Try this at home with your own "Random Acts of Kindness Chain." It is a great reminder that the smallest acts can sometimes make the biggest difference.

82

Birthday Donations

• • •

When my son turned one I was overwhelmed by the number of presents he received. Between family, friends and my husband and me, he received enough presents to fill a small warehouse. It was mind boggling and disturbing at the same time. I tossed and turned that night trying to decide how to handle the balance between wanting my child to enjoy his birthday while not raising a spoiled-rotten child.

There are many different ways for children to give back on their special day. You can ask for a donation on your child's birthday invitation instead of presents. Each year you can decide on old toys to be donated to make room for new toys. Instead of buying party bags, you can make a donation in honor of your child's favorite charity. As your children become older leave it up to them to make the decision.

Giving back to others is such an amazing lesson to teach our children. So while they might not receive as many gifts on their birthday, they will receive a much bigger gift as they grow, the gift of giving.

83

Gratefulness Jar

• • •

The older I become the more I am convinced gratitude is what makes the world go around. Grateful people create happy people and happy people create a happy world. Therefore, wouldn't it make sense to teach our children the joy of being grateful?

Not too long ago my cousin shared with me how she and her family celebrate gratitude. She has a beautiful jar sitting on a countertop stocked with paper and pens. When someone is feeling grateful he writes his feelings on a piece of paper and places it in the jar. At different times in the month the family opens the jar and read what they have written.

Create your own "Gratefulness Jar" and teach your children the joy that comes with being grateful.

84

Dinnertime

• • •

Life gets busy and schedules get full, but making time for family dinners is a must. It is a time to teach manners, discuss life and just be a family.

Schedules have become so busy with extra activities that parents have completely forgotten how important dinnertime is. If you find your children eating dinner on the couch with the television on, music in their ears or staring at a computer screen, it is time to come back to the table.

Kids today mainly communicate through text messaging. I never thought I would hear myself say that talking is becoming a thing of the past, but it is. Without verbal communication, kids are losing a sense of empathy for others and are not in touch with reality. Dinnertime is more important than ever.

While at the table, talk about everyone's day and get some sort of discussion going. If you are at a loss for conversation there are a number of great dinnertime questions for families and conversation starters online. One of my favorites comes from www.tabletopics.com.

For younger kids I recommend Ian James Corlett's book, *E Is for Ethics: How to Talk to Kids About Morals, Values, and What Matters Most*. This book is filled with cute stories about ethical issues that are wonderful conversation starters.

I can guarantee that your children will have no recollection of the television show they were watching while eating dinner on the couch, but they will remember the dinnertime conversation you shared. Most importantly, you will be teaching your children how to communicate with others without pushing buttons and staring at a little phone screen.

85

Lessons from the Library

• • •

I love the library. It is a place where children can learn responsibility and respect. Having been an elementary school teacher, I not only love children's books, I have a lot of them. My children would read through these books and before I knew it they were piled up in every room. It was time to teach my children the art of respecting books. This is when we started taking trips to the library.

Give each of your children a bag to hold their library books, get them each a library card and begin going once a week to return old books and check out new ones. If they end up with an overdue charge, they are responsible for the payment. If they harm the book, they are responsible for the damage.

The library is also a place where moms can teach the respect of calm and quiet like no other. If a child is throwing a temper tantrum in the library, he will stick out like a sore thumb. Because the library is a "quiet zone" children tend to learn by example. Those who are usually rambunctious take it down a notch because of their surroundings.

Last but not least, the library is a great place to do homework when you have extra time between activities. My children sit down and complete their homework immediately because then they have more time to look at books.

Teaching children to respect and love books is a true gift. I strongly believe that reading is one of the fastest ways to develop a curious and knowledge-filled mind. There is nothing like finding a moment of quiet to escape into the lives of so many others and learn something new in the process. Check out your books, read together as a family and enjoy watching your child's mind grow. What a blessing.

86

Field Trips

• • •

How many endless hours have you spent at those wonderful, money-sucking, sugar-overloading, pizza joints? It seems like an amazing place for moms, because, while the kids run around and play moms get to check out mentally. The problem is that the kids leave wired from all the video games, ticket-eating machines, soda pop drinks and noise, spending the rest of the day melting down and whining.

Why not try something different? There are so many wonderful places you can take your children. Think of these places like the field trips your children take at school.

Every state is filled with places that children would find fascinating and they are usually educational as well. If you research your own area you would be surprised what is available. In my state, there is a candy factory, a teddy bear factory, a police museum and a butterfly pavilion, to name a few. Every week the newspaper is filled with different places you and your family can experience.

You get to be with your family, your kids get to experience something new and the rest of the day won't be filled with meltdowns and temper tantrums. Everyone wins.

87

Picked Especially for You

• • •

There is nothing more endearing than opening a gift from a child and watching his face glow with pride. I will never forget when I received a rabbit candlestick holder from my daughter. It was nothing I would have picked for myself, but that rabbit sat on my kitchen windowsill for as long as I can remember. Teaching our kids at a young age to pick out presents for others is an important lesson. They learn early the wonderful feeling of giving to others and there is a pride that comes with choosing the gift all by themselves.

A while back I took my daughter to the store and had her pick out Christmas gifts for her grandmas, her grandpas, her dad, her brother and her sister. The one thing I told her was to think of each person and what they love to do. After that she was on her own. I followed her around with a basket as she talked through each gift. "Grandpa likes to garden so I will get him this shovel. Papa likes to do dishes so I will get him a sponge. I will get Grameese this plate because she likes plates. Here is a pink basket for Magga. She likes pink." We bought the gifts and headed home to wrap them. On Christmas day, she beamed with pride.

So as birthdays and other holidays come and go, let your kids be part of the process. It is sometimes easier to do it yourself, but then the actual point of giving is lost in the hustle and bustle of life.

88

Needs vs. Wants

• • •

We seem to be a society of wants—I want an iPod; I want a bigger house; I want what she has; I want, want, want! Not too long ago I was watching a television show where the discussion was how humans are the only creatures using more than they need. Somehow we have correlated happiness with wanting more, when in reality wanting more can sometimes leave an endless pit of unhappiness.

Talk with your children about needs versus wants. When you go to the store to buy milk and eggs, you are supplying needs for nourishment, but when you buy candy these are things you want. When we buy school clothes, these are things we need, but buying a pair of shoes when we already have five pairs is a want.

Needs help us survive and wants are extra. There is nothing wrong with wanting, but overdoing wants is wasteful. Understanding the difference between needs and wants will teach our children the value of simplicity.

89

What Are Your Kids Watching?

• • •

Children today are seeing, learning and experiencing more at an earlier age than any other generation. The television shows our children are watching are partially to blame.

A few years back I sat down to watch television with my children. They were watching a show on what was supposed to be a "kid's channel." My then nine, seven and three year old were learning how to date, kiss and call their teacher stupid all in one episode! Here I was trying to teach my children how to be respectful, caring and well behaved and within one thirty minute show everything I taught went out the window. It would be one thing if they watched this once in a while, but they were choosing this as their television almost every night. I was in such need of a mommy break that I completely ignored what my children were watching. I began checking out their other shows of choice and realized that these were no better than the first.

Shows like these are affecting children more than most parents realize. Robert Shaw paints a not so pretty picture of television's affects on children in his book, *The Epidemic: The Rot of American*

Culture, Absentee and Permissive Parenting, and the Resultant Plague of Joyless, Selfish Children. Shaw claims that television is affecting children's neurological, psychological and emotional development. The amount of television our kids are watching, as well as what they are watching is causing these developmental problems. Does this mean we throw away television for good? No. Shaw believes that "media in moderation" is what is needed to help reverse the affects of too much television and inappropriate television.

After I realized the shows my kids were choosing seemed to be less than appropriate, our family sat down for a chat. My husband and I explained why we disagreed with the shows they were watching and we offered alternatives. Believe it or not, our children were okay. They did not throw fits or run away. They enjoyed their new choices. I am not naive in thinking that my children will never watch these shows at a friend's home, but I feel much better knowing that they are watching them once a month rather than every day.

90

The Game of Life

• • •

Sports are a microcosm of real life, but that microcosm can burst if parents don't stand back and allow these life lessons to unfold. There will be times that our child will miss the winning goal. There will be times that our child will be benched for yelling at the referee. There will even be times our child will not make the team. With the exception of physical or mental abuse from a coach, it is important to take a step back from our emotions and allow our children to work through these moments.

My son began playing soccer at a very young age and was playing club soccer by the time he was in second grade. From almost the beginning he was voted in as one of the team captains. During his fourth year a new coach took over the team. Four other boys received the captainship and my son was devastated. I could have gone to the coach and asked why my son wasn't chosen and I could have complained that I thought he should have been, but I didn't. I told my son that sometimes he would be top dog and other times he would not. If he really wanted to be captain he needed to work hard and prove himself. He ended up having an amazing year and learned a valuable lesson in the process.

Be there as a support, but let life happen. Be your child's best advocate, but do not get in the way of his lessons. These lessons will help mold children into adults who are able to deal with whatever comes their way.

91

Simple Birthday Parties

● ● ●

When you hear the words, "Birthday Party," what goes through your mind? For some moms it is a wonderful thing, but others dread the thought of planning their child's party. First, there is the list: who will be invited, who will be left off the list and who will have hurt feelings? Then, there are the expectations: where will it be, how much will it cost and will everyone like it? Many children's birthday parties have become productions that are not about the children, but keeping up with the Joneses!

At the other extreme we have moms who just want to sign on the dotted line and have nothing to do with the planning. I am the first to say that I have been this mom. Why? Because it is easy. The facilities do everything from the activities to the food, cake and party bags. They even supply you with the invitations and thank you notes. While moms have the best intentions, wouldn't it be nice to make our children's birthdays unique? What happened to the days of simple parties at home?

Not too long ago I went to a birthday party at a friend's home. There were about ten children: they swam, played a few games, ate watermelon and corndogs, sang happy birthday, ate cake and left with a homemade music CD. Simple, simple, simple. The kids had a blast, they did not leave over-stimulated or jacked-up on sugar and the party was inexpensive. The best part—it was all about the birthday boy. Isn't that what birthdays should be about?

92

Creative Play vs. Commercialized Play

• • •

When I was teaching I loved watching the kids on the playground. They were princesses of their castle, animals deep in the jungle, soldiers conquering the bad guys or mommies and babies playing at the park. They could create magic with nothing but their imaginations.

Today we see play morphed into something else—less imagination and more commercialism. It is now Cinderella© and Belle© in their castles, Dora and Boots© going through the jungle or the Power Rangers© conquering the bad guy. Children are not creating their own stories, but following the script they know from television or the movies.

Spontaneous play is important for children. Play is tied to impulse control, brain development and emotional development. While it is virtually impossible to completely stay away from commercialism and the toys our children play with, we do have some control. When you are buying toys for your children, consider the oldies but goodies: blocks, plain Legos©, trains, generic dolls, dress up clothes and good old Crayola© crayons. Do your child a favor—help him get back to playing with some imagination.

93

The Allowance Dance

● ● ●

A few years back I bought three jars for each of my children. I put a label on each jar and wrote spending on the first one, savings on the second and charity on the third. Each week we would give our children their allowance and they would divide their money between the three jars. We felt it was a great way to teach our kids about money. The problem was we always forgot to pay up. Life gets busy and allowances always ended up on the back burner.

Recently, I was lucky enough to come across www.threejars.com. This is a website that tracks kids' allowances, teaches them about managing their money and makes paying children easy. Who knew clicking the mouse could be so helpful teaching our children about money?

94

Guess the Cost

● ● ●

When we were kids our parents would make the comment, "Money doesn't grow on trees." Today we have these things called ATMs that children think hand out money like it is candy and credit cards that magically buy things for us. If we don't explain money to our children they will grow up thinking they simply push some buttons or slide a card and they will get whatever they want.

Play a guessing game whenever you are paying a bill. Whether it is eating at a restaurant, buying groceries or going to the movies, have each child guess how much the bill will be. Their guesses might be way off, but with time they will understand that things are not free, ATM's aren't magic and credit cards are not just for swiping.

95

A Dollar a Day

• • •

Waiting, waiting, waiting. This word can make a child crazy. The instant gratification world that we live in is damaging to our children's development of impulse control. We need to teach our children the art of waiting.

I can remember being a child and saving my pennies, nickels, dimes and quarters in my piggy bank. I would empty it out, count how much I had and think about what I was going to buy. Kids today don't seem to have as much patience when it comes to money.

Buy a glass jar and label it a "Dollar a Day." Every day pick something that your child can do to earn $1, nothing more and nothing less. Put the dollar in the jar and watch it grow. After a month take the money out and count it. After two months take the money out and count it. By the time six months rolls around he will have earned almost $180. That is definitely more than I ever had in my piggy bank.

A "Dollar a Day" can help teach your children to appreciate the time it takes to earn and save money. What a great tool to learn at a young age.

96

Perfect is Boring. Be Yourself.

● ● ●

Families might look like everything is perfect on the outside, but that is not always true. Striving for perfection puts a lot of pressure on us as well as our children. In our family I like to say, "Perfect is boring, be yourself." There are times that you might see me and my family and everything is running smoothly: the kids are groomed; we are laughing; my children are being polite; and life seems good. On another day you might see the total opposite: my youngest is melting down in the middle of the grocery store; my two older kids are fighting; hair brushing was optional for the day; and I have a scowl on my face that I just couldn't peel off if I tried.

My point is, cut yourself some slack and don't judge how well you are parenting based on what another family looks like on the outside. Just because things look perfect doesn't mean they are. We spend way too much time feeling good or bad about our own parenting skills based on what other families are doing.

As the old saying goes, you can't judge a book by its cover. Some-one else's book might look wonderful on the outside, but you have no idea what their story is on the inside. Create your own cover, as well as your own story, with all of the ups and downs that come with raising a family. In the end you will have taught your children that creating your own story is priceless.

97

Quiet Time for Mom

• • •

Lately I have heard statistic after statistic about how dangerous it is to be driving while talking or texting on the cell phone. Researchers are saying it is just as bad as driving drunk. Once I heard the statistics I decided it was time to make a life change. I no longer use my phone while I am driving. The hardest part was seeing how dependent and addicted I had become. I quickly realized how much time I was spending checking texts, emails and voicemails almost without consciousness. Looking back, I am sure if I had videoed myself in the car I would have been dumbfounded. Kids asking me questions. Me half hearing them and half responding to them because I was driving one-handed while chatting with my friend about who knows what. This followed by my kids screaming at me because I was so checked out—all while I was driving. I definitely would not have won any mommy awards at that moment. Yet moms are doing this everyday, all the time.

My car is now a different place. Not too long ago I was driving alone, my cell phone was turned off and the radio was not playing. It was like nothing I had heard in a long time—silence. At first I was a little antsy, like an addict needing a fix. But as time has passed, I look forward to those quiet moments.

We spend so much of our time in the middle of noise. Try turning it all off and spend some time without it. You might be surprised how peaceful it can be and at the same time you will be safer on the road.

98

The Mother-in-Law

• • •

I am not a big fan of assumptions, but for right now I am going to make some. I assume if you are reading this book you have or will have children. I assume that if you are reading this book there is a strong chance that some day your children might marry. If the last assumption is true then some day you will be a mother-in-law. Seems kind of strange doesn't it? If you have daughters, our society tends to keep them close to their family of origin, but if you have sons our society tends to pluck them from their family of origin and plop them into their wife's family of origin. If you are the mother of a son take a deep breath and read on.

When your husband was a boy, his mother meant the world to him, just like your son means the world to you. When your husband was a boy he turned to his mother for everything, just like your son turns to you for everything. As time went on, your husband grew and needed his mother less, but his mother never forgot the love they shared. More time passed and you came into your husband's life, fell in love and married. The man you married is still the boy whom your mother-in-law raised and loved, just the way you are raising and loving your son.

If you have a son, I want you to ask yourself one question, "Are you treating your mother-in-law the way you will want to be treated when your son is married some day?"

If you have a wonderful relationship with your mother-in-law, keep it up. If you don't and you are raising a son, realize that you will be in her shoes someday. Pick up the phone and give her a call. Putting ourselves in someone else's shoes can sometimes open our eyes to a world that is closer to home than we realize.

99

On Separate Pages

$\bullet\ \bullet\ \bullet$

One of the easiest ways to create a house of chaos is to have two parents on different pages. Kids can sniff out EVERYTHING! Even if you think you are hiding your differences, most likely it is seeping through at some level. No matter how well you organize your house and yourself, no matter how much you know about parenting, no matter how much you try your hardest, if you and your husband, partner or significant other are on separate pages, your kids will take those pages and shred them.

Does this mean you can't have differences of opinion? No. Those differences need to be respected and discussed without the children around. Your children need to see a strong unit standing together and respecting one another.

What happens when one person tries to move a piece of furniture, while someone else pushes against them on the other side? The furniture is impossible to move. You might as well put all the kids on top of the furniture and watch them laugh as you push against each other. On the other hand, what happens when two people work together to move a piece of furniture? It moves. The kids might try to sit on the furniture to stop it from moving, but soon they will realize it is easier to help push than go against it.

Sit down together and discuss what your plan is for parenting. When your children see that they cannot break your bond, they will stop trying.

100
Date Night

• • •

This is not earth shattering, but something we as parents always seem to put last on our list is date night. Date night is not only important for parents to get the time they need together, but it is also important for the kids. When they see you putting effort into your relationship it gives them the security to know they have a mom and dad who love one another. It also lays the foundations and expectations of what their relationships might look like in the future. So while they might give you a hard time as you are walking out the door, it fills everyone up in the end.

Last But Not Least

• • •

As I bring this book to a close, I find myself hoping that it has brought a glimmer of hope to those feeling the most strung out, a glimmer of help to those feeling a little strung out and a glimmer of happiness for those not feeling strung out at all. We are all at different points on the road of parenting. No matter what phase you find yourself in, remember that another phase is right around the corner and another one and another one and another one until finally you have given your children the tools they need to take on the world. Whether you use one idea from this book, one hundred ideas or something in between, my hope is that parenting becomes a little less crazy—at least most of the time.

References & Recommendations

● ● ●

Bronson, P.O. & Merryman, A. (2009). *Nurture shock: New thinking about children.* New York, NY: Twelve.

Brown, S. (1964). *Flat Stanley.* New York, NY: Harper-Collins Publishers.

Chua, A. (2011, January 8). Why chinese mothers are superior. *The Wall Street Journal.* Retrieved from http://online.wsj.com.

Corlett, I. J. (2009). *E is for ethics: How to talk to kids about morals, values, and what matters most.* New York, NY: Atria Paperback.

Dobson, J. C. (2009). *Bringing up girls: Practical advice and encouragement for those shaping the next generation of women.* Carol Stream, IL: Tyndale House Publishers.

Dweck, C. S. (2006). *Mindset: The new psychology of success: How we can learn to fulfill our potential.* New York, NY: Ballantine Books.

Greenspan, S. I. (2002). *The secure child: Helping our children feel safe and confident in a changing world.* Cambridge, MA: Da Capo Press.

Gurian, M. (1996). *The wonder of boys: What parents, mentors and educators can do to shape boys into exceptional men.* New York, NY: Jeremy P. Tarcher/ Putnam.

Johnson, M. A. (2001). *Positive parenting with a plan: Grades K-12.* Anchorage, AK: Publication Consultants.

Leman, K. (1998). *The birth order book: Why you are the way you are.* Grand Rapids, MI: Revell.

Peck, M. S. (1978). *The road less travelled: A new psychology of love, traditional values and spiritual growth.* New York, NY: Simon & Schuster.

Shaw, R. (2003). *The epidemic: The rot of American culture, absentee and permissive parenting, and the resultant plague of joyless, selfish children.* New York, NY: Regan Books.

Stamm, J. (2007). *Bright from the start.* New York, NY: Gotham Books.

www.threejars.com

www.flylady.net

Thank You

● ● ●

I would like to thank to my editor, Ami King. Without your guidance and friendship, *DiddleDots* might have made its way back to the dusty shelves. You were able to clear the clutter and find my vision hidden in the jumble of words and thoughts.

To Chris Klonoski, thank you for helping me start the process. You were instrumental in helping me organize *DiddleDots*.

To my counselors, thank you for helping me peel through the layers. Without you *DiddleDots* would never have been created. I am forever grateful.

To my friends, thank you for being in my life. To the world you might be one person, but to this person you are the world. Thank you for your love and support.

To the DEARS, the outlaws, the cousins and the Garlicks, I love you 10,000 times more than you love me. How blessed I feel to be part of such an amazing family.

To my mom and dad, thank you for standing by me. The beauty of a rainbow only shines after a storm. What a beautiful rainbow we have created. I love you.

To Ryan, Macy and Kenzie, there are no words to express the love I have for each of you. You make me laugh; you make me cry; you make me real. I love you to the moon and back, again and again and again...

To Mike, for twenty-three years you have been my rock, my cheerleader and my best friend. Thank you for walking next to me, holding my hand and teaching me what love truly is.

• • •

DiddleDots can be purchased at

www.amazon.com

A portion of the proceeds will go
toward children's charities.

• • •

Join the conversation at

www.diddledots.com